Developing

AKING ORGANIZATIONS MORE H

Innovating
Innovation

Catalyzing your leadership practice

Publisher's note

Every effort has been made to ensure information contained in this publication is accurate at the time of going to press. Neither the publishers nor any of the contributors can accept responsibility for any errors or omissions, however caused, nor for any loss or damage occasioned to any person acting, or refraining from action, as a result of the material in this publication.

Users and readers of this publication may copy portions of the material for personal use, internal reports, or reports to clients provided that such articles (or portions of articles) are attributed to this publication by name, the individual contributor of the portion uses and publisher.

IEDP Ideas for Leaders Ltd
42 Moray Place, Edinburgh, EH3 6BT
www.ideasforleaders.com

in association with the Center for the Future of Organization at the
Drucker School of Management
www.futureorg.org

Publishers: Roland Deiser and Roddy Millar
Editor-in-Chief: Roddy Millar
Senior Editor: Roland Deiser
Associate Editors: Saar Ben-Attar (Africa), Suzie Lewis (Europe)
Conrado Schlochauer (LatAm), Ravi Shankar (SE Asia)
Art Direction: Nick Mortimer – nickmortimer.co.uk

Copyright ©2024 IEDP Ideas for Leaders Ltd and contributors

ISBN 978-1-91-552924-4 (Paperback)
ISBN 978-1-91-552925-1 (e-Pub)
ISSN 2044-2203 (Developing Leaders Quarterly)

www.developingleadersquarterly.com

Contents

There is nothing new about innovation. We are only living the technologically advanced lifestyles we do today because humans have been innovating constantly for millennia. Innovating is a peculiarly human thing to do – we may get excited when we see a crow using a stone to raise water levels in a glass, or a chimpanzee using a stick to reach ants (Google them!), but this just highlights how little animals innovate. The rate of innovation change, with humans, has increased dramatically though in the last 200 years – and in the 21st century it will be a key, if not *the* key, factor in determining successful organizations from the laggards.

In this issue of *Developing Leaders Quarterly* we examine what is needed to enable innovation to happen. As always in DLQ, we explore the topic through the lens of organizational leaders, and with our definition of leadership to the fore. That is 'leaders are those who create the conditions for others to do their best work, in pursuit of a common objective' (leaders also do vision and strategizing, but that is a much smaller percentage of their activity, although more glamorous and inevitably more focused upon).

Andy Binns's opening article highlights the difference between innovators as founders in start-ups and those tasked with innovating in established organizations, his 'corporate explorers'. Understanding these differences is hugely important, and Andy shares his huge experience with us *on creating the conditions* for those explorers to flourish. Our second insight comes from Helmut Schönenberger and colleagues at **UnternehmerTUM**, the Munich-based start-up accelerator, where they describe the conditions of collaboration and support they have created to amazing effect to make UnternehmerTUM the leading European start-up initiative. **Fernanda Carapinha**'s article puts the financial backers under-the-spotlight, and notes that it serves men better than women, and salesmen (of their ideas and businesses) best of all – at the expense of those who have innovative ideas and thinking, but less ability at pitching, and asks if this is really the optimal context for gaining innovation.

Silicon Valley has been the cradle of innovation this century and largely set the rules for how it has been done. So, **Agustin Couto**'s piece, with colleagues, on his time leading **Facebook/Meta**'s Learning & Development in Latin America, and creating the conditions for innovation to take place, not just in that organization but with their customers too, is an enlightening read. Our final innovation focused piece is from **Michael Nichols** who brings his years of practical experience at **Bosch** and now **Mann+Hummell**, where he is director of Corporate Ventures, to examine what makes for successful conditions to innovate in organizations – with the resounding conclusion "ultimately, innovation is a people and leadership challenge."

Beyond the realms of innovation, but not unconnected to it, **Colin Mayer**, the former Dean of Oxford Saïd Business School, writes about the role of the corporation in resolving our largest global challenges, and the argument for devolving responsibilities to lower levels of the organization, and creating greater agency and purpose, to enable firms to sustain and adapt and do the right thing. **Marsha Ershagi** and **Maria Colacurcio** take this theme forward, making the case for more data, and so greater transparency to improve workplace equity.

We close with a selection of eclectic pieces, **Bernie Jaworski** and **Victoria Cheung** connecting the dots between the wisdom of Confucius and that of Peter Drucker, with some powerful insights for modern-day leaders from ancient practice. **Alexander Mackenzie** takes the use of ancient oriental practice onwards with his use of mandalas and storytelling as the basis for 'big picture' leadership. And **Ingrid Pope** closes this issue with some practical steps to keep all this information and more in accessible order by implementing de-cluttering best practice.

As always, we hope you find the content both broad and deep and that it provides you with the catalysts for moments to reflect that will enhance and support your own leadership.

Roddy Millar, Editorial Director and Co-publisher
Roland Deiser, Co-publisher

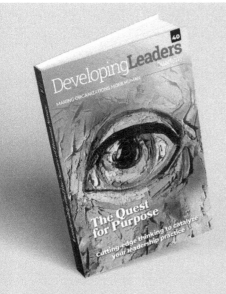

Thinking imprinted.

The first step on any leadership development process is to create space and condition for reflection on your leadership practice.

Multiple studies have concluded that we absorb and digest information better when we read off the printed page. Reading is focused, uninterrupted and, with the chance to note down our own thoughts in the margins, print allows us to actively engage with the subject.

To embed the change, Developing Leaders Quarterly is best in print.

Developing Leaders Quarterly print edition is ideally formatted to slip into your pocket, bag or briefcase to read when you find you have a few minutes to spare before a business guest arrives, while commuting, at the airport...

SUBSCRIBE AT DEVELOPINGLEADERSQUARTERLY.COM/SUBSCRIBE

By Andy Binns

The Hidden Power of Corporate Explorers

nnovation is misfit in many corporations. CEOs want to be more innovative, but high costs and high uncertainty tend to make them cautious. Corporate innovation teams lose the battle for resources and attention to slower growing, more profitable operating businesses. Corporations periodically try to fix this problem by developing processes, methods, and tools to support innovation. This has led to the phenomenon of the innovation theatre; high levels of activity that translate into little change in innovation outcomes.

The alternative strategy is to hire an entrepreneur from outside the corporation to lead the charge. In the popular imagination, entrepreneurs are synonymous

Most successful corporate innovation projects are led by long-time managers from inside the firm. The challenge is to find them and give them the opportunity to succeed

with innovation. The famed, if not always admired, leaders of Amazon, Google, and Tesla have truly rocked our world. It is therefore logical for CEOs to look outside their organizations to lead new ventures. However, this may not be the most effective strategy; in fact, most successful corporate innovation projects are led by long-time managers from inside the firm. The challenge is to find them and give them the opportunity to succeed.

In my work, I have looked at the career trajectories and innovation projects of dozens of successful and unsuccessful corporate innovators. I have found that meeting the challenge of finding entrepreneurial talent inside an existing corporation means setting aside some of the biases in how we define and evaluate leadership in corporations. Corporate Explorers, as I like to call them, are systematically disadvantaged by talent management processes and leadership competency models that are premised on what it takes to develop leaders for an operational business.

Disruptive technologies, like AI, machine learning, and a host of other digital innovations create opportunities beyond the core business that can generate the sort of growth CEO's want to achieve. It is one thing to reduce marketing costs by applying ChatGPT or improve operational efficiency with digital twins, but these technologies have much greater potential. Converting these opportunities is the real game – one that will require leaders with the capability to incubate and scale new businesses. These are leaders with an entrepreneurial, not operational, skill set.

If we are going to be serious about developing these exploratory leaders, we need to be able to: (1) accept that

Two-thirds of executives appointed from outside the company to lead innovation projects leave their jobs within three years.

insiders are a source of entrepreneurial talent, (2) appreciate what differentiates these leaders versus managers of an operational business and external entrepreneurs, and (3) reimagine talent management for the purpose.

Insider or Outsider?

When GE's former CEO Jeff Immelt initiated the company's digital transformation in 2013, he followed a familiar pattern of finding a skilled executive from outside the company to lead his new "Predix" business. Bill Ruh was hired in from Cisco Systems, where he had had a very successful career, particularly leading the transition from being an telecoms equipment company to one that sells IT services. Ruh had everything on his side. He had the explicit backing of the CEO and board of directors and a public commitment to making GE a "top 10 software company." However, five years later, both Immelt and Ruh had left the company, and the strategy was cancelled.

Although there are many reasons for the failures at GE, Ruh's fate does represent a repeating pattern. In our research, two-thirds of executives appointed from outside the company to lead innovation projects leave their jobs within three years. In contrast, when we examine innovation projects that succeed, they are in many cases led by experienced insiders, often with more than 10 years tenure in the company.

These Corporate Explorers can be found in multiple industries and across the globe, for example:

- **LexisNexis** – Jim Peck went within 10 years from being a middle manager in its news and legal information business to the CEO of a new multi-billion-dollar big data unit.
- **UNIQA Insurance** – Krisztian Kurtisz went from managing the relatively small Hungarian business to creating a new digital-only business, transforming the company's value proposition and operating model across countries.
- **AGC** – Hideyuki Kurata has built a new contract pharmaceutical research and development business. Ventures such as these started in 2015; they now account for 25% of the company's profits.
- **Deloitte** – Balaji Bondili developed "Deloitte Pixel" which reinvented the professional services labour model by using crowdsourced talent to work along-

side employed consultants, with a billion-dollar impact for the company.

- **Atlanta Opera** – Tomer Zvulun reinvented opera in the middle of the COVID pandemic, making it possible to perform when all other opera houses were closed.

These are real, contemporary examples of innovation successes that should make CEOs trust that they can find innovators from within their own management ranks. The challenge is to recognize them.

What is Different about Corporate Explorers?

Larger, more established firms tend to have some sort of formalized talent management process for assessing the potential of key managers and deciding how to progress their careers. BCG says that a leadership team should spend 30-40 days per year on talent management. Most of this time is focused on how to develop people for leadership within the existing core business – the large P&L, sales, operational, and functional jobs in the company. These are complex responsibilities, and most companies struggle to have enough candidates for the positions they need to fill.

The profile of the leader of a small, unproven venture is entirely different from that of the manager of a stable, mature operating one

The challenge is that the profile of the leader of a small, unproven venture is entirely different from that of the manager of a stable, mature operating one. Operational managers are effective at managing large numbers of people toward goals within areas in which the parameters of performance are known and understood. There are processes, key performance indicators and metrics, that they can monitor to detect variance to plan and adapt accordingly.

Explorers have few of these operational guideposts. They are operating in a new market without a performance track record or deep knowledge about customer behaviour. They need to manage high uncertainty to actively eliminate these risks before advocating that the business invests in the new venture. This is not a mini-general management role; it is a completely different skill set.

There are three key differences between the core business leader and the innovation leader.

Innovation leaders are explorers.

Businesses at different stages of maturity require different approaches. A mature, relatively stable franchise needs someone able to dig into the operational levers of performance to squeeze out a few additional points of margin, even as they delight customers with on-time delivery and quality. A new business is all about instability, trying different approaches, pivoting quickly, and staying focused on the long-term. This requires a bias for exploration, a drive to understand what is changing in the world, rather than how to make things predictable. That is why I call them Corporate Explorers.

Peter Robertson at Nyenrode University in the Netherlands has demonstrated how a bias toward exploration or stability is hardwired into us as a prod-

A new business is all about instability, trying different approaches, pivoting quickly, and staying focused on the long-term. This requires a bias for exploration.

uct of evolution. That means that Corporate Explorers tend to be regarded as misfits inside organizations that have a strong bias towards delivering predictable results. They may be good corporate citizens, perhaps even trusted performers, but they do not fit the mould when it comes to big business unit leadership roles. They are regarded as a little wild or unconventional. It is exactly these characteristics that make them good at managing the uncertainty inherent in an immature, developing venture.

Corporate Explorers are curious about unsolved customer problems.

The most common "origin story" for a corporate venture is a Corporate Explorer who observes something in the world that they feel the rest of the business is missing. At UNIQA, Krisztian Kurtisz believed traditional insurers were ignoring younger, urban dwelling consumers who were digital natives that had not developed the habit of signing-up for insurance policies in the traditional way. At

Deloitte, Balaji Bondili had tired of the consulting grind on the road every day and wondered why firms like his could not adapt their labour models to attract a wider pool of expertise in domains such as machine learning and artificial intelligence. This curiosity turned into a quest to solve the problem and build a new business.

This characteristic is also found in entrepreneurs. Amy Wilkinson in her book the "Creator's Code" says entrepreneurs are "gap closers." They see something in the world that does not work right and that inspires them toward constructing a solution. She explains how Jack Ma was a teacher in a provincial Chinese high school when he spotted a gap in e-commerce. Ma noticed that small and medium sized Chinese companies had no route to market online, so he created Alibaba, a company now valued at over $200 billion.

Corporate Explorers are similar. They have the explorer's insight about the gap in the market. The project to develop this insight to a new business offering becomes a personal quest. However, their motivation often comes from a sense of personal frustration. Kurtisz was frustrated with the slow speed of digital adoption in the insurance industry as well as the high costs and poor service it imposed on consumers. Bondili believed consulting could do better work for clients and give its team members a better lifestyle.

Corporate Explorers set a high ambition.

Corporate Explorers set a level of ambition equal to the opportunity or threat of disruption, rather than to what is most achievable. Tomer Zvulun, General Director of The Atlanta Opera, exemplified this characteristic in his response to the coronavirus pandemic. In March 2020, as the scale of the pandemic emerged, Zvulun cancelled the entire season. All other opera companies in America and around the world did the same, accepting that live performances would not return until public gatherings were permitted.

Zvulun saw it as his duty to bring hope to his audiences and the local artistic community. Within a month, he had committed the company to the ambition of reimagining opera in a way that would allow them to perform. This would mean keeping all participants safe yet retaining the ability to emotionally inspire audiences and create a commercially viable business model.

He adopted an agile innovation methodology to rally his team to solve the myriad problems involved in staging live opera in the middle of a global pandemic. He was told repeatedly by his team and many experts that what he wanted to be achieved could not be done. However, by October 2020, the Molly Blank Big Tent Series launched, with thousands of Atlantans treated to performances of live opera in a custom open-

What was remarkable is how the Corporate Explorers let others take credit for what they had achieved. It did not matter whether this reflected reality; what was important is that they built support by making these leaders feel they had a stake in the success of the venture.

sided tent in a college baseball field. This made The Atlanta Opera the only opera company in the country, and one of only a few worldwide, to perform live and safely during this period. Zvulun's vision was realized because of his passionate commitment to an ambition and dogged determination that inspired others to overcome the barriers.

How are Corporate Explorers Different to Entrepreneurs?

These three characteristics – exploratory, curiosity, and ambition – are significant in explaining the difference between leading innovation and leading core business operations. However, they are roughly similar traits to those that we see in entrepreneurs like Musk, Jeff Bezos, and others. We cannot understand the essence of the

Corporate Explorer without also appreciating the differences between them and founders of start-up ventures.

The key differences are humility and social influence.

Corporate Explorers demonstrate humility.

Multiple studies have demonstrated a link between entrepreneurship and narcissism. That means that they lack empathy toward others, yet have a great need to be admired, coupled with a strong sense of self-importance, even entitlement. This is somewhat intuitive given the self-belief required to sustain an idea through many rounds of investor rejection. One unpublished study of Silicon Valley start-up founders suggests that narcissism is the only one of the "big five" psychology traits that distinguishes successful from unsuccessful entrepreneurs.

The toughest task for the Corporate Explorer is to align the organization around the new venture.

Corporate Explorers on the other hand need to demonstrate humility if they are to win support inside the organization. When I was doing the research for the book *Corporate Explorer: how corporations beat start-ups at the innovation game*, I interviewed both the innovators who had led successful corporate ventures and the executives who had sponsored them. What was remarkable is how the Corporate Explorers let others take credit for what they had achieved. It did not matter whether this reflected reality; what was important is that they built support by making these leaders feel they had a stake in the success of the venture. It helped them be perceived as trying to realize an opportunity to solve a valuable customer problem, rather than pushing a particular product or technology.

Humility is vital to helping the Corporate Explorer navigate the choppy waters of winning and sustaining senior leadership support. It makes it possible for the new venture to be coded as a shared goal, rather than a pre-determined agenda to aggrandize the individual advocating the innovation.

Corporate Explorers build social influence.
The toughest task for the Corporate Explorer is to align the organization around the new venture. New ventures often start out with strong support, riding the wave of the latest technology or business model trend. However, until the venture has tangible evidence that it is going to work, it is an unproven cost to the business, and support ebbs away as the slow, steady work of validating the venture with experiments starts.

Almost by definition, new ventures face internal organizational resistance as they challenge the assumptions about how traditional business is done. Consulting companies pride themselves on recruiting and developing the best consultants in the industry. When Bondili proposed hiring them on a project basis via a third-party platform it sounded like heresy. Kurtisz broke the rules of insurance by offering monthly subscriptions and guaranteeing the payment of claims without verifying them first. Zvulun took opera into a tent and put singers inside plastic cubicles to allow them to sing without a mask.

It takes a high-level of social influence to overcome these barriers. It requires strong relationships with others in the organization, people who will speak-up for the venture when it is discussed at internal meetings. Corporate Explorers cultivate support from these allies and advocates. They are not solo performers, but people

Finding Corporate Explorers is not the same as appointing a new "head of innovation" or R&D leader. You need to create opportunities for Corporate Explorers to step forward and make a case for the problem that they believe the company should invest in solving for a customer group.

who identify with the company's culture and purpose. This is where external hires are at a big disadvantage. They come in to challenge the fundamentals of how business is done, as Bill Ruh did at GE Digital, but have no social influence in the organization. This makes it very hard to overcome the resistance to change that exists in any successful, incumbent organization.

How do we find Corporate Explorers?

These five characteristics – exploratory orientation, curiosity, ambition, humility, and social influence – are what differentiate successful Corporate Explorers. Knowing these can help you recognize potential innovators, even when they do not fit the standard definition of a general manager or other senior leader in an organization.

Here is where you need to challenge a traditional talent management assumption that people are given new roles. Most Corporate Explorers create the opportunity themselves. There was no leadership position advertised at UNIQA for digital value propositions, for crowd-sourced talent models at Deloitte, or big data risk analytics business at LexisNexis. These three Corporate Explorers built the opportunity themselves, with the help and support of a cast of allies and advocates.

That means finding Corporate Explorers is not the same as appointing a new "head of innovation" or R&D leader. You need to create opportunities for Corporate Explorers to step forward and make a case for the problem that they believe the company should invest in solving for a customer group. There are several options for how to do this.

- **Provide a License to Explore** – there is a great disconnect in many organizations between CEOs that are frustrated at getting too few proposals for how to build new businesses and managers who believe the corporation is risk averse, unwilling to back innovators. Corporate Explorers need to believe that they have a license to explore. CEOs can signal this in how they talk about the company's strategy. At Analog Devices, the $90 billion-dollar market cap technology company, CEO Vincent Roche announced his strat-

*These five characteristics –
exploratory orientation, curiosity,
ambition, humility, and social
influence – are what differentiate
successful Corporate Explorers.*

egy as being to "move up-the-stack" and serve more complex customer problems. He invited his managers and engineers to propose how they would do this. This has created multiple new growth engines for the company, including its software defined radio franchise that has powered the adoption of 5G mobile networks around the world.

- **Create a formal process** – Companies like Robert Bosch GmbH and Siemens Factory Automation invite teams in R&D to propose new ventures and bring them into a formal "Validation Engine." This is a step-by-step approach to validating the customer problem that the team believes they can solve by engaging in up to 100 interviews with potential users and buyers. The process is so rigorous that over 90% of teams voluntarily conclude that their idea will not fly. The few that succeed have real evidence that they address a problem that customers will pay to solve.

- **Use informal processes like executive education** – A rigorous validation engine model can be resource intensive. Another way is using executive education programs to enable high-potential managers to develop new concepts. For example, Federico Spagnoli, CEO of Prudential's "Total Wellness Solutions" business, first developed his concept on a business school strategic innovation program. The structure of the program enabled him to formulate his thinking and get senior executive attention that provided his initial seed funding.

Leveraging the innovation potential of Corporate Explorers rests on the premise of helping them to "step forward" rather than making top-down appointments. This is a

Leveraging the innovation potential of Corporate Explorers rests on the premise of helping them to "step forward" rather than making top-down appointments.

challenge to traditional human resource practices, but it is essential to capture the difference between finding high potential explorers and high potential operators.

Start-ups will always have an edge when it comes to attention and glory. They get to give their new companies funky names, announce funding rounds, and get new listings on stock exchanges. However, beneath this froth there will be Corporate Explorers working more quietly, who are able to build new value propositions for existing corporations. Those corporations that can identify and encourage their entrepreneurial talent to emerge will put themselves in a stronger position relative to both competitors and startups.

Andrew Binns is managing principal of Change Logic, a Boston-based strategic advisory firm. He is co-author of Corporate Explorer *(Wiley, 2022) and co-editor of* The Corporate Explorer Fieldbook.

By Helmut Schönenberger, Christian Mohr & Jennifer Kaiser-Steiner

Innovating Innovation

The Entrepreneurial Ecosystem of Munich's UnternehmerTUM

Today's world is characterized by challenges and uncertainties, such as climate change and the associated environmental disasters as well as resource scarcity, military conflicts, inflation, and political instability. The dynamics unleashed by these crises are changing the economy and the way how value chains and cooperations work worldwide. In addition, new technologies such as artificial intelligence and cloud computing are having a major disruptive impact on all business models.

In this rapidly changing and increasingly demanding global context, companies and nations have to prove their competitiveness and ability to innovate time and time again. Creating continuous innovations is a must if we want to ensure a sustainable, prosperous and progressive society in the future.

With their ability to react quickly to new circumstances, start-ups are in particular a driving force for innovation. Universities play an important role as a source for talent and technological innovation. With the right mechanisms, insights and solutions from research can be quickly introduced into practice via start-ups so that cutting-edge technologies become new products and services, and tangible value is created from academic research. In addition, start-ups have become an increasingly indispensable innovation source for established companies, which are eager to collaborate and engage in entrepreneurial partnerships.

Munich's UnternehmerTUM – a Benchmark Innovation Ecosystem

In our experience, the key to promoting innovation and new technologies lies in creating a dynamic network that connects the stakeholders who are instrumental for success: established companies, universities and research institutions, start-ups and politics. Designed

Creating continuous innovations is a must if we want to ensure a sustainable, prosperous and progressive society in the future.

well, such a network will create a strong business cluster. Co-operation across cluster boundaries is crucial for economic success.

The Munich metropolitan region is an excellent example of such an innovation ecosystem which is well designed and utilized. With top universities such as the Technical University of Munich (TUM) and Ludwig-Maximilians-Universität (LMU), non-university research institutions like the Max Planck Society, global businesses like BMW, Siemens, or Infineon, and a large number of agile tech start-ups, Munich has become an attractive location for top international talent. The enriching interplay of competition and strategic cooperation creates a unique ecosystem that promotes and drives innovation. In this dynamic environment, UnternehmerTUM – the entrepreneurship center at TUM – acts as an enabling platform for the various players.

Since its founding in 2002 by German entrepreneur and BMW heiress Susanne Klatten, UnternehmerTUM has established a systematic spin-off process to bring innovative companies to the global stage and attract key players in the technology sector. Over the years, it has grown to become the largest start-up and innovation center in Europe. Today, the entrepreneurship center employs over 400 people (FTE) and supports more than 50 high-growth technology start-ups per year, making it a key player in the European innovation arena who provides an important contribution to a dynamic start-up ecosystem.

In 2022, the influence of TUM and Unternehmer-TUM reached a new benchmark: over 20 percent of Germany's venture capital volume – more than 2 billion euros – flowed into start-ups supported by these institutions. Notable success stories include unicorns such as Celonis[1], Lilium[2], Flixbus[3] and Personio[4], all of which are part of this success story.

---

1 With 3000+ employees and a valuation of $13bn, Celonis is the global leader in process mining, providing companies a modern way to run their business processes entirely on data and intelligence – www.celonis.com.

2 Lilium is an emissions-free regional air mobility service which has developed the first electric vertical take-off and landing jet – www.lilium.com.

3 Flixbus is a unique combination of tech-startup, e-commerce platform, and transportation company, featuring 400,000 daily connections to 3000+ destinations in 40+ countries – www.flixbus.com.

4 Valued at about $9bn, Personio provides an all-in-one HR software solution that upgrades people operations for business up to 2000 employees – www.personio.com.

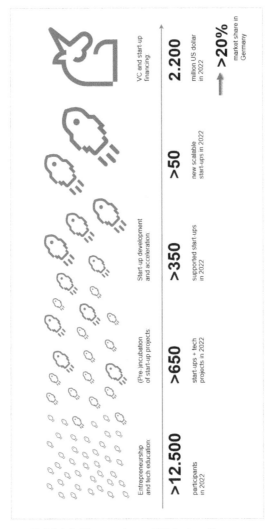

Exhibit 1: UnternehmerTUM – key figures

UnternehmerTUM transcends traditional funding structures and offers a comprehensive range of activities for individuals at all stages of the start-up process. From hackathons and makeathons to talks and seminars, the organization promotes a hands-on approach that provides aspiring entrepreneurs with practical insights and experience, supporting entrepreneurial minds throughout their entire start-up journey.

The roots of this success lie in a collaborative ecosystem that brings together companies, SMEs, universities, research centers and service providers in and around Munich. This powerful network not only facilitates innovation; it also creates synergies: large companies benefit from the inventive spirit of start-ups, while start-ups find ways to expand through strategic partnerships with established companies.

The City of Munich, the Bavarian State Government and the Federal Government have recognized the central role of UnternehmerTUM and TUM as leading entrepreneurial institutions. This has led to a close and productive partnership at various levels to jointly shape the future of technological innovation and the success of start-ups. For example, as part of its national innovation strategy the German government intends to build 10 more startup factories in Germany – under the role model of and in collaboration with UnternehmerTUM.

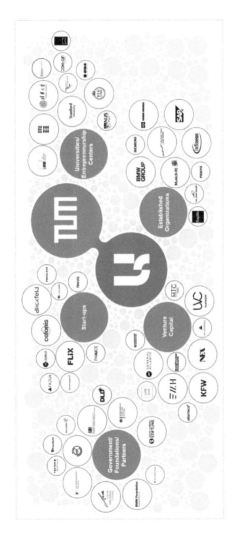

Exhibit 2: Stakeholders of the UnternehmerTUM Innovation Ecosystem

Tackling the challenges of today

Considering the big challenges business and society are facing, the need for sustainable innovation has never been greater. Responding to this need, Unternehmer-TUM has set up in recent years several initiatives to bring about innovations for economic and social change.

Circular Republic

One important area of innovation we address in this context is Circular Economy. As we grapple with the

As we grapple with the drawbacks of a linear economic model that proves to be inherently unsustainable, the call for a transformative shift towards a circular economy has become increasingly evident.

drawbacks of a linear economic model that proves to be inherently unsustainable, the call for a transformative shift towards a circular economy has become increasingly evident.

The circular economy redefines our approach to consumption and production by promoting sustainable practices such as sharing and recycling. Shifting to this model benefits both industry and society by conserving natural resources, reducing waste and emissions, and creating novel economic opportunities.

Companies that embrace the principles of the circular economy benefit from efficiency, cost reduction and increased competitiveness. Start-ups, with their innovation and agility, play a crucial role in driving this change.

For this reason, UnternehmerTUM has launched the **CIRCULAR REPUBLIC** initiative with corporate partners such as BMW, Prezero, SAP and Tengelmann. CIRCULAR REPUBLIC serves as a catalyst for sustainability, from electric cars to recycling innovations. Start-ups such as Made of Air and FINN are contributing to the circular economy.

Venture Labs

Another initiative are the **TUM Venture Labs** that are designed to further promote and expand the translation of cutting-edge research into marketable applications. TUM Venture Labs support TUM scientists and students even more deeply in the spin-off of companies in various technology-based fields at the interfaces of engineering, natural and life sciences, artificial intelligence, and medicine, offering founders a comprehensive ecosystem with the necessary development environments. The offer ranges from technical and social infrastructure such as workplaces, laboratories and workshops to entrepreneurship training and support from a network of companies, mentors, investors, and scientific experts.

Leading deep tech start-ups to success requires a deep understanding of the focus technology, which is why we created Venture Labs in various deep tech verticals. Eleven Venture Labs have been set up since October 2020. They work in the areas of software/AI, robotics, quantum, aerospace, built environment, chemistry, healthcare, food/agro-biotech, additive manufacturing, mobility and sustainability/circular energy economy.

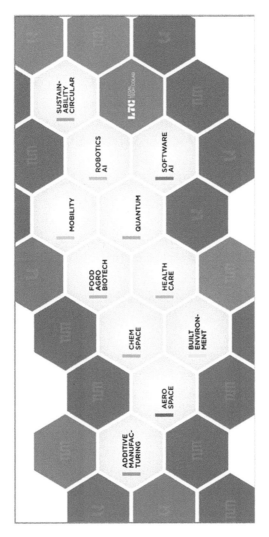

Exhibit 3: Technology Verticals of the TUM Venture Labs

In the second year since its foundation, about 250 start-up teams are already being supported by the Venture Labs. This way, the labs create dynamic ecosystems from which not only individual companies can emerge, but also entire start-up families. The initiative aims to strengthen cooperation with other universities and also become a model for startup creation at German universities.

Focus on the Family

Germany is known for its "Mittelstand", with its hidden champions and family businesses. They make up a large part of the national value creation and economic growth, and they must remain innovative as a backbone of Germany's industry. After all, family businesses generate over 50 percent of Germany's gross domestic product.

FamilienUnternehmerTUM, one of the focus fields of the entrepreneurship center, has set itself the goal of strengthening German SMEs and thus contributing to Germany's innovative strength and prosperity for future generations. The initiative aims to closely network SMEs with start-ups and the research community in a pragmatic and output-oriented way. By teaming up, digital transformation and especially the application of artificial intelligence as well as the adaptation of new technologies get implemented faster and more efficiently. Roadshows, scouting and matchmaking

Participating companies are exposed to hundreds of other innovators, researchers, students, and entrepreneurs and receive new inspirations by connecting to an interdisciplinary community.

programs, accompanied pilot projects and joint financing and scaling efforts support the joint value creation process.

At UnternehmerTUM, family businesses not only find start-ups and other established companies as collaboration partners. The entrepreneurship center with its infrastructure and community is also a space for experimentation. Participating companies can send their innovation teams to the our facilities and be part of the creative work environment. They are exposed to hundreds of other innovators, researchers, students, and entrepreneurs and receive new inspirations by connecting to a interdisciplinary community. This meeting-market and deal-making environment leads to a continuous flow of new joint innovation projects and ultimately win-win success stories.

In an era characterized by interconnected global economies and shared environmental challenges, collaboration across national borders has become essential.

Rise Europe

In an era characterized by interconnected global economies and shared environmental challenges, collaboration across national borders has become essential. Achieving both economic prosperity and environmental sustainability requires concerted efforts and collaborative partnerships between key players in the innovation system. In this context, Rise Europe is an important initiative.

Launched in May 2023 by UnternehmerTUM, DTU Skylab and the Paris-based incubator Agoranov, Rise Europe is a pan-European network composed of leading developers of start-up ecosystems. The mission of this collaborative effort is to promote European start-ups and provide them with the support and resources they need to thrive in a competitive and dynamic landscape. With representatives from 14 European countries, Rise Europe seeks to accelerate the growth of start-up teams

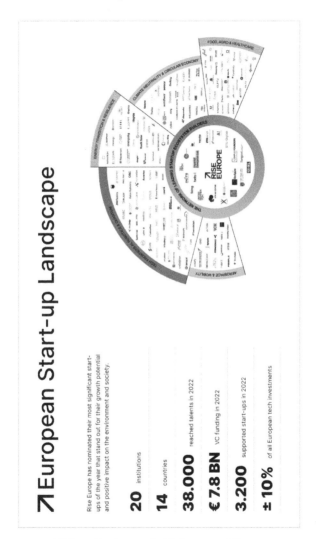

Exhibit 4: RiseEurope's high-potential start-ups

The idea behind these efforts is to inspire the next generation to think and act entrepreneurially across national borders.

and contribute to the development of European technological sovereignty.

At its core, Rise Europe is dedicated to tackling critical transitions and global challenges, including the climate crisis and resource scarcity. By supporting start-ups who are committed to creating a safe, prosperous, and future-oriented society, the network aims to make a significant impact at both a regional and global level. Through a combination of strategic initiatives, mentorship programs and access to an extensive network of resources, Rise Europe strives to position European start-ups as catalysts for positive change.

The members of the Rise Europe network are united by a shared commitment to pool their strengths and create an environment where innovation thrives. The goal is to match the innovative power of the United States and China and to bring European start-ups to the forefront of the international scene. Rise Europe aims to reshape the history of European entrepreneurship and contribute to the continent's economic and technological leadership by facilitating their scaling-up and transforma-

tion into sustainable global leaders. In doing so, we strive to create a legacy of innovation that transcends borders and shapes the future of the global start-up ecosystem.

The numbers speak for themselves: In 2022, Rise Europe's 20 European start-up hubs inspired a total of 38,000 young talents and students across Europe to start their own businesses, and they supported 2,300 up-and-coming ventures in their development phases. The idea behind these efforts is to inspire the next generation to think and act entrepreneurially across national borders.

Rise Europe's shared platform concept enables founders to benefit from a diverse range of resources and offers. With a total of 7.8 billion euros invested in the supported start-ups, these 20 European entrepreneurship centers make a significant contribution to the economic vitality of the European start-up scene. This amount of funding corresponds to around 10% of total investment in the European tech industry.

The members of Rise Europe have each nominated ten start-ups that they believe have the greatest potential to become the next "start-up champions" . These scale-ups – including *Fernride* from Germany, *IQM* from Finland and *Ynsect* from France – are characterized by their growth and a positive impact on the environment and society. The nominees have been assigned to four fields, reflecting the potential that Europe has in these future areas: aviation and mobility, artificial intelligence and robotics, energy, climate neutrality and circular economy, and health and food (see exhibit 4)

This overview underlines the importance of the European start-up scene and the influence of the 20 members of Rise Europe. The recent publication of the European Start-up Map is a further step towards a more connected and thriving European start-up scene. In addition to striving for greater visibility for Europe as a start-up hub, the members of Rise Europe want to join forces with industry, family offices, political institutions, and investors to improve the environment for entrepreneurial initiatives in Europe and provide start-ups with easy market access to talent, customers, and capital across Europe.

Outlook

Start-ups, characterized by their speed, adaptability, and privileged access to cutting-edge technology, play a central role in promoting innovation and the rapid market introduction of new products and services. Recognizing the potential of start-ups as engines of economic growth and technological advancement, there is a growing emphasis on creating an environment that encourages and supports entrepreneurial initiatives, especially those emerging from higher education institutions.

If we want to strengthen the entrepreneurial ecosystem and facilitate the seamless transition of spin-off teams from academia to industry, we must professionalize existing support structures and processes. This includes developing comprehensive frameworks that provide guidance, mentoring and resources to these burgeoning start-ups and ensure that they navigate the complexities of the business landscape with confidence and competence.

But this alone is not enough. The optimization of the transfer of intellectual property from universities must

be accompanied by a stronger financing landscape in Europe. Such a financial infrastructure is a key success factor when it comes to developing new European innovation champions. To achieve this, it is important that more venture capital is made available for start-ups in Germany and Europe, for example by unlocking financial resources from insurance companies, pension funds or foundations.

UnternehmerTUM started out as a regional Bavarian initiative, supported by an influential and wealthy entrepreneurial visionary. From the outset, it followed an emphatic network strategy, connecting entrepreneurs,

If we want to strengthen the entrepreneurial ecosystem and facilitate the seamless transition of spin-off teams from academia to industry, we must professionalize existing support structures and processes.

academia, government, established business, and funding sources, and providing a unique development and support infrastructure for start-ups. Today it towers as a global benchmark of an innovation ecosystem which has few, if any, peers. With Rise Europe the journey now enters a new, exciting level: the ambitious and important project of raising the full entrepreneurial potential of Europe which will create a new generation of market and technology leaders.

Helmut Schönenberger *is co-founder and CEO of UnternehmerTUM and VP for Entrepreneurship at the Technical University of Munich.*

Christian Mohr *is Managing Director and CCO of UnternehmerTUM and an expert on family-owned companies.*

Jennifer Kaiser-Steiner *is responsible for partnerships with ministries, universities and start-up factories at UnternehmerTUM.*

www.unternehmertum.de/en

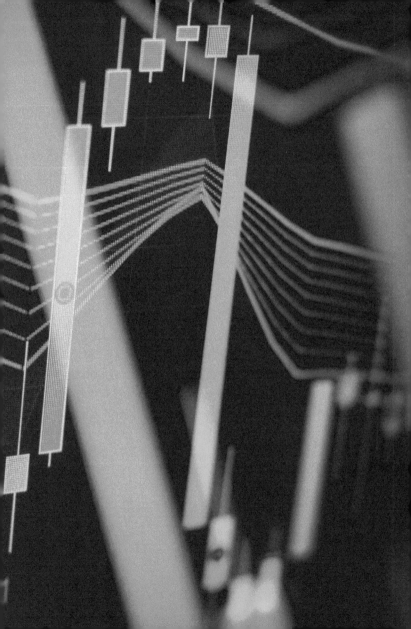

By Fernanda Carapinha

Revolutionizing Emerging Business Growth

Today's start-up ecosystem abounds with resources specifically tailored for women: women-led VCs, women-focused Angel Networks, professional women's entrepreneurial organizations, incubators, accelerators, coaches, and a variety of government and private grants for women-led businesses. Despite this comprehensive range of support, which has been growing for years, a pivotal question arises: what has been the impact?

Exhibit 1[1]

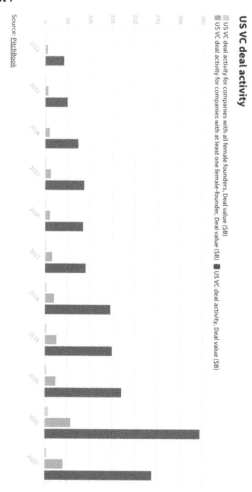

US VC deal activity

US VC deal activity for companies with all female founders, Deal value ($B)
US VC deal activity for companies with at least one female-founder, Deal value ($B)
US VC deal activity, Deal value ($B)

Source: PitchBook

---

1 Source: Pitchbook, quoted in www.linkedin.com/pulse/
bridging-vc-funding-gap-supporting-women-people-color-entrepreneurs/

Funding of female-led start-ups has not increased; in fact, it has decreased from 2021 to 2022.

An analysis of the investment activity of US based Venture Capital reveals that funding of female-led start-ups has not increased; in fact, it has decreased from 2021 to 2022 (see the pink bar in Exhibit 1). There is some growth with mixed male and female teams (purple) but there is little transparency on what that really means from an equity parity perspective. Although there are more female-led teams numerically, male-led startups receive 98% of the funding.

Why, despite all the efforts to increase funding to women, is the needle not moving? What is the root cause that lies behind the lack of opportunity for female founders to get a bite at the success apple? To answer this question, let's first take a closer look at the current paradigm of the entrepreneurial support system.

A Broken Paradigm

Funding for women and underrepresented founders is undoubtedly crucial. However, our intense focus on this issue makes us blind to the bigger systemic factors driving disparities. In 2022, approximately six thousand

Imagine if these were the statistics for higher education, where 99.9% of all degree-holders were unemployed. We would be scrutinizing the system failures, not the individuals.

companies exited globally; if half were led by women, it would be a significant achievement. Yet, it would merely be a drop in the massive ocean of failure that engulfs the universe of founders, and that goes largely unnoticed.

Consider the numbers: in 2022, 50 million businesses were founded globally. An astonishing 90% of these emerging businesses fail. Only 10% (5 million) manage to reach a VC's door, and less than 1% secure funding, nearly all of which goes to male-led teams (98%). Of those funded, 75% eventually fail. In the end, only 25% of these companies experience an exit via IPO or acquisition (exhibit 2). Less than a tenth of a single percent of entrepreneurs ever witness their companies exit, from the top to the bottom of the funnel, making the industry's focus on this tiny sliver of success both myopic and misguided.

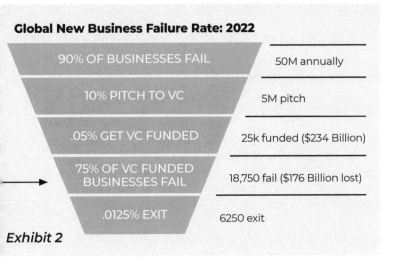

Global New Business Failure Rate: 2022

90% OF BUSINESSES FAIL	50M annually
10% PITCH TO VC	5M pitch
.05% GET VC FUNDED	25k funded ($234 Billion)
75% OF VC FUNDED BUSINESSES FAIL	18,750 fail ($176 Billion lost)
.0125% EXIT	6250 exit

Exhibit 2

Imagine if these were the statistics for higher education, where 99.9% of all degree-holders were unemployed. We would be scrutinizing the system failures, not the individuals. The solution would not involve aiding the 1% in finding jobs – yet that is analogous to what we do in the entrepreneurial ecosystem. We focus on fixing problems at the bottom of the funnel, while neglecting the massive collateral damage that precedes it. No number of "Find Your Bliss" workshops can plug this hole.

We are sacrificing millions of entrepreneurs to find the few because no one has committed to fixing the real pipeline problem. There is no ground zero talent development mechanism, no life-cycle business development infrastructure, and an over reliance on a single business model (equity financing) to drive an entire industry. The innovation business is not designed by innovators but by financiers and bankers who often lack operational experience.

How did it come to this?

The Misguided Focus on Funding

In the past, entrepreneurs primarily bootstrapped their ventures, building them from scratch with minimal external capital. This was often not a choice but the only viable option. Success took decades, not just five years.

The emergence of venture capital transformed this landscape, allowing entrepreneurs to secure funding much earlier in their journey, often with little revenue. This shift gave rise to an industry centered around the pursuit of capital. "Getting funded" became synonymous with entrepreneurship, altering the way businesses were conceived, developed, and scaled. The amount of funding raised became a badge of honor, validating a venture's value proposition, strategy, financials, and team.

However, the equity-business model that dominates today's discourse has steered everyone towards the metaphorical "Cinderella funding ball," an exclusive event led by venture capitalists in search of the elusive unicorn. VCs may invest in 100 companies, hoping for around 10 profitable exits. If just one becomes a unicorn, their financial goals are met.

"Getting funded" became synonymous with entrepreneurship, altering the way businesses were conceived, developed, and scaled.

Investors in VC funds expect substantial returns, usually within five years. In this equation, the nature of your product or service takes a back seat. Your venture becomes primarily an investment vehicle, where world-changing impact is welcome but not essential. This reality often escapes us as creators and visionaries. Investors, even those aligned with our mission, want to know how we will make them money first. They antici-pate significant returns, typically 3-5x in the early stages and up to 8-10x by the fifth year.

In this "survival of the fittest" game, failure is not an anomaly; it's a part of the process. It is even desired because the natural elimination of weaker companies saves time and resources. The system does not prioritize building an entrepreneurial talent pipeline; it aims to find natural-born unicorns amidst the chaos. The problem is not Venture Capitalists nor their business model, it is that everyone else in the ecosystem who wants to transform the system has blindly adopted this bottom of the funnel infrastructure upon which to build a better tomorrow.

The failure principle may work well for Limited Partners and institutional investors, whose funds are aggregated into one large VC fund. Here, a portfolio strategy mitigates risk and allows the sharing of upside among investors. However, for founders who have staked their homes, left their jobs, and risked financial security to chase their dreams, there are no such risk management tools. This is why we created the WEscore – the first early-stage emerging business holistic risk assessment tool that benefits both founders and investors, because who wouldn't want more exits and unicorns in their portfolio?

The Under-appreciation of Revenue

While founders diligently engage in training sessions, courses, coaching programs, incubators, and accelerators – all meticulously designed to help them perfect their investor pitches and secure funding or become 'investor-ready', the vital necessity of becoming *'revenue ready'* – the critical piece of any business – often remains overlooked. Their intense quest for investment can veil the fundamental task of building a robust, scalable, revenue-generating foundation for their businesses—full stop.

This funding-centric, Darwinian approach leaves a gaping hole in the system. Where can novice entrepreneurs, lacking initial resources or connections, find long-term development support? Unfortunately, the answer is often nowhere. The world of founders desperately needs a development-focused infrastructure guiding talent from ideation to achieving $2 million in revenue. This milestone signifies successful navigation through the 'valley of death' and unlocks new opportunities.

Adding complexity to the journey towards sustainable revenue is that raising capital involves enduring a barrage of 'no's' before finally receiving a 'yes'. Most rejections leave entrepreneurs without valuable feedback, compelling them to grope in the dark for improvement strategies. Without the benefits of connections, experience, and a solid track record, failure is an all-too-frequent outcome.

An estimated 80% of business success is driven by psychology – the inner work – while only 20% depends on operational expertise and knowledge – the outer work.

If we aspire to increase the number of successful ventures significantly, we must radically rethink our approach. Instead of congregating at the (funding) water booth at mile 25 of the marathon, where everyone currently focuses, we need to move to the start of the race to drive real systemic change so that hundreds of thousands of global companies exit at the bottom of the funnel not just a few.

We must design various business models aligned with the long-term progression of entrepreneurial talent. We must build a new solid development pipeline for millions of founders, guiding them through the valley of death. In other words, we must create an infrastructure equipping entrepreneurs with tools and guidance from the very beginning of their journey, even if it takes years.

Bottomline: we need a sophisticated ground-up architecture to craft a new innovation ecosystem that produces high quality talent and startups that puts revenue generation not equity at its center. Investor interest is a natural byproduct of building a successful business. This is what we are building at WE Global and what we are committed to achieving.

Building A Woman's Founder DNA™

This brings us back to the unique entrepreneurial challenges that women face. While there are many, I'll highlight five key points.

The Psychology of Success

Lack of confidence, fear of failure, and ingrained negative beliefs often hinder a founder's success. Overcoming these internal barriers is vital. Women are often raised in the *Risk Petri Dish* of life while men in the *Opportunity and Abundance Petri Dish* (there are historic reasons for that – a topic for another time). We still carry all that legacy computer programming in our subconscious, which we are often oblivious to, and we do not recognize how it cripples our success. This is what I call mastering the Radical Center™, where psychology, the psyche, and business intersect. An estimated 80% of business success is driven by psychology – the inner work – while only 20% depends on operational expertise and knowledge – the outer work. This is why *Building Founder DNA* is our first and most crucial pillar of excellence at WE Global.

Network and Social Capital

Many women lack access to valuable networks and do not have experience leveraging social capital that can fuel business growth. Some women's organizations even

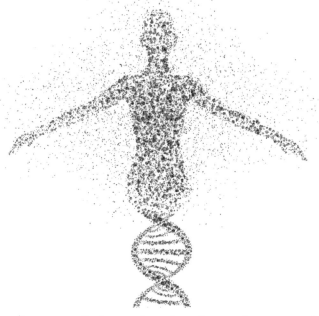

discourage their members from leveraging connections for business purposes. We have dedicated an entire hub at WE Global to facilitate connections of all types.

Blind Navigation

Navigating the entrepreneurial journey for women and underserved founders can feel like being dropped into the wilderness with minimal supplies in your backpack, no map, and a big ticking clock because friends and family funding is smaller, runway shorter and family pressures mounting. The terrain is fraught with threats (bad advice, untrustworthy partners, business roadmap void) – and meanwhile the challenge is to collect milestones to prove your worth. This journey underscores the need for operational and systematic tools, resources, and strategic step-by-step guidance. This is why we created WE Copilot, the first AI business partner, that helps emerging businesses assess and bridge business gaps. This ungated end-to-end platform provides all the essential resources in one place, supporting navigation of the entrepreneurial journey.

Exclusive Gated Outposts

While some resources exist within exclusive gated communities (incubators, accelerators and VCs), access can be challenging and temporary, and diversity is often lacking as we have stated above. We have taken an inclusive approach at WE Global, offering a SaaS model and a non-profit arm to ensure access for all interested founders.

Not Speaking the Language

Just like anything else, business has its own language – and it is called finance. Whether it is understanding the cost of capital, knowing how to build a financial model and leverage it, managing your P&L, and negotiating deals – founders need to become financially savvy. This is an area many women do not have experience in. This blind spot has deep roots that start back in school with girls and math. This lack of expertise is compounded when stepping into the bootstrap world. Here you find the best kind of capital, your revenue, but you must master the language of finance. Learning to master this game, despite its high risks, can be fueled by entities that understand the process. That is why we created the *WEscore*, the first AI-driven risk assessment platform. It examines the six progressive tracks that take you from ideation to scaling, assessing and minimizing risk for founders while building and scaling their businesses. It benefits founders, investors, and all stakeholders.

WE Global Studios: Innovating the Innovation System

The dysfunctionalities of the entrepreneurial world and the challenges entrepreneurs face open the space for innovating the innovation system. Enabling technologies such as Web3, the changing nature of work, and the rabid appetite for entrepreneurship, make the field of emerging business growth ripe for massive disruption.

WE Global Studios has been created for this purpose – to dismantle traditional barriers for founders by getting them access to an infrastructure that provides a comprehensive portfolio of support mechanisms.

At its core WE Global is an AI-data analytics platform, focused on assessing and mitigating the growth of businesses globally. It offers, among other features, two key

Business has its own language – and it is called finance. Whether it is understanding the cost of capital, knowing how to build a financial model and leverage it, managing your P&L, and negotiating deals – founders need to become financially savvy.

solutions that are designed to strengthen Founder DNA and enable sustainable emerging business success: The *WEscore* and the *Founderverse*.

The WEscore

The *WEscore* is a risk assessment solution that provides objective and unbiased holistic feedback to founders about their current capability gaps and recommends a focus on specific problem areas before these gaps become a liability. This is critical, because founders rarely get meaningful operational and business development feedback at the early stages before they have millions in revenue, because of their limited networks. If they pitch VCs and are passed on, they do not receive any substantive guidance beyond the cursory; you are too early, not a thesis fit; don't see how this scales. Hence, how do founders get better? They often do not and the numbers reflect that.

The *WEscore* assesses six major tracks, 36 sub-tracks, 60 micro-tracks and examines hundreds of data points. The six tracks include:

- **Building Founder DNA** – assessment of founders and their team
- **Business Strategy** – review of the strategic, foundational and market research work that is imperative before investing in product development
- **Product Development** – best practices.
- **Marketing & Sales plan** – strategies and progress
- **Operations** – infrastructure and execution
- **Scaling viability and strategy**

The goal is to holistically look at strengths and weaknesses in a non-punitive fashion and pass the founder on to the next part of WE Global, the *Founderverse*, where founders can mitigate and improve those weaknesses. The scores are dynamic and meant to coach and guide. High scores unlock privileges and access to non-dilutive sources of funding.

The Founderverse

The *Founderverse* is a massive ecosystem with centralized activity hubs that guide founders to the appropriate mitigation solutions. At its core lies a comprehensive AI-driven analytics platform with a multi-sided ecosystem which brings together not just founders and funders but also customers, service providers, universities, other ecosystem players, and non-dilutive sources of funding – on one tech platform that is truly scalable.

The architecture of the *Founderverse* is dedicated to driving traction, emphasizing the growth of revenue, user engagement, and the cultivation of partnerships and customer relationships. A major cornerstone is a focus on developing leadership talent – both for founders and their extended teams. In essence, founders can leverage a one-stop support infrastructure that helps them construct their companies meticulously, with the resilience and preparation needed to thrive under the pressures of scaling.

More than 250 founders are already part of WE Global Studios, and their number is rapidly growing. By using the *WEscore* to better understand their strengths and weaknesses, and by leveraging the support infrastructure of the *Founderverse*, their businesses will have a better chance to grow and to succeed. In their aggregate, they are pioneering our answer to the shortcomings of an innovation industry that should and can do better.

Fernanda Carapinha *is a serial tech entrepreneur and the Founder and CEO of WE Global Studios.*

www.weglobalstudios.com

By Agustin Couto, Kelsye Gould,
Gian Taralli, and Jason Wisdom

Hacking Our Way to Innovation

How Facebook reimagined its client relationship practices and helped global brands to innovate

An Insider's Look at What Drives Innovation

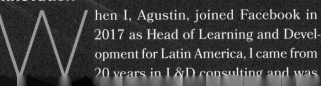

When I, Agustin, joined Facebook in 2017 as Head of Learning and Development for Latin America, I came from 20 years in L&D consulting and was

Facebook had a strong culture based on collaboration, experimentation, and focus on impact. There was a tacit expectation that individuals and teams should fail from time to time because, "if you're not failing, you're not growing."

accustomed to serving large corporations to elevate their teams' skill level. I was used to delivering transformative learning programs to change business practices for targeted teams inside large organizations, but I had not yet managed system-level change. By becoming an an insider in a large corporation like Facebook – as opposed to an outside consultant – I had more leverage to influence multiple teams at once through an extended period of time. As I was to discover, it would grant me the opportunity to drive systemic transformation, especially in an organization that had peculiar characteristics that, I can tell in hindsight, were key ingredients to drive innovation.

The first thing that struck me when joining Facebook was the elevated skill level and talent of the people that worked there. It was not uncommon that people left director-level positions in large banks, telecoms or consulting firms to be senior account managers at Facebook. Renowned leaders in top advertising agencies would join the Creative Shop team, mathematical geniuses would leave academia to join the Marketing Science hub. Over a few years, this led to a highly talented pool of driven people that wanted to perform the best work of their careers. This was great, but not necessarily conducive to innovation on its own. The fact that we had very talented individuals did not mean they would together undertake productive work and build the required relationships. It is a well – known fact that a team composed of stars does not necessarily win the championship.

This is where culture kicks in. Facebook had a strong culture based on collaboration, experimentation, and focus on impact. There was a tacit expectation that individuals and teams should fail from time to time because, *"if you're not failing, you're not growing,"* and an expectation that you should also produce breakthrough achievements from time to time

When you have talented, driven individuals embedded in a culture like that, you get an organization that can collaborate and drive a lot of change. Hackathons, in which teams would get together to solve a specific challenge, were a common practice. Although teams were used to collaborating and producing amazing results, Hackathons were mostly technically oriented, focused on improving results on Facebook's advertising platform. When involving clients, collaboration projects would revolve around improving the execution of their digital marketing campaigns, optimizing ads, systems integration or the creative aspect of digital ads, generating results specifically to the marketing team responsible for digital campaigns within clients. They were not innovating in Facebook's go to market approach, its commercial practices, or in the way they related to clients.

To learn the business, I would sporadically shadow sales professionals to client calls. Every time I did it, I was impressed with the high level of trust they had earned from their clients, the world's largest brands. Through diligent work over a few years of serving the same book of business, the commercial teams had positioned themselves as trusted advisors: clients would listen to them attentively and, very often, follow their recommendations. Facebook was a small size operation in Latin America when compared to its clients; yet they had significant influence over their decision making in regard to digital marketing and advertising.

Despite their high level of influence over clients, at the end of 2017, the commercial team was facing a critical challenge: they had committed to another year of intense growth, but there was no clear path to accomplish it. For the past three years, the Latin American Facebook team had been driving hyper-growth, moving from being the slowest to the fastest growth market globally. This led them to take most of the digital advertis-

ing budget available in the market, and they started to plateau. There was no clear way to generate new or additional revenue streams to sustain the committed growth. We had hit saturation.

That was the moment the Vice President of Facebook LatAm and the Head of Sales LatAm came to me asking for some type of learning intervention that could make the teams more strategic in their approach to the market. The idea was to make teams go beyond their traditional way of doing business and start tending to broader client needs. If we were to keep growing at high rates, we needed to start addressing client challenges that would involve new, more elaborate and larger advertising solutions. In other words, we needed to innovate.

As Head of Learning, I knew that offering one more traditional training would not cut it. The solution needed to transform our way of working, leveraging the trust clients had in Facebook's culture of open experimentation. We needed an innovative, hands-on approach to get Facebook *go to market as a strategic enterprise team*. To create such an approach I needed help, and that's when I reached out to The Design Gym, a consultancy specialized in that field.

The Innovation Hacking Program

Painting the Vision

When designing a strategic engagement approach for Facebook's most important clients, it helps to imagine what these clients would say after a successful experience. Ideally they would say things like "The Facebook team is our chosen partner to lead innovation in the way we advertise." Or "Facebook helps us move things forward.", "They have a definite seat at our strategy meetings."

With this ambitious vision in mind, the Design Gym team embarked on a robust discovery process. To better understand the needs of Facebook teams and their clients, they interviewed 30 internal and external stakeholders and reviewed past client surveys.

From this research, they learned that although advertising clients generally had a positive relationship with Facebook, the nature of that relationship tended to be more *tactical* and *transactional* when, in fact, they were looking to Facebook to be more of a *strategic* and *consultative* partner. They wanted their conversations to shift from media pitches to advising on business growth and market trends.

However, the sales environment was already challenging due to greater competition, increased quotas, and dwindling "low hanging" opportunities. Asking Facebook teams to deliver on clients' growing expectations while also serving as strategic partners required more than shifting how they worked with clients. It required the organization to shift how it evaluated success from short-term quotas to creating long-term value.

The cross-functional nature of the program is a markedly different way of working for Facebook's customers. In fact, for some of them it was their first time working across the aisles.

It became clear that a solution that any innovative design that addresses these expectations had to help Facebook teams:

1. Understand their customers' perspectives and needs;
2. Look for challenges that are meaningful to their customers;
3. Consider solutions that feel innovative to the client; and
4. Create a team mentality around the client challenge.

With these insights and design principles in mind, as well as inspiration from Facebook's history of technology Hackathons, the team designed a customer engagement program called *Innovation Hacking*.

Innovation Hacking is an approach for quickly and collaboratively creating marketing plans and initiatives that are consumer-centric, actionable, and mutually beneficial. It consists of three phases:

1. **The Challenge Phase** – understand the context surrounding the client's problem and reframe the challenge accordingly.
2. **The Ideas Phase** – create innovative solutions and prioritize a range of short, medium, and long-term ideas to test.
3. **The Action Phase** – align with the client on the ideas to test and implement.

Learning by Testing

In the spirit of Design Thinking and iterative learning, the program was piloted with two Facebook customers in Brazil. To test the approach in different organizational cultures and industries, two different types were selected for the pilots. One was an e-commerce company that was known for being innovative. The hypothesis was that they would be more open to experimenting with a new approach. The other one was a more traditional company in the beauty industry with whom Facebook had already established trust but wanted to grow the relationship. Here, the hypothesis was that the initiative would help realize a greater potential to generate more business with the client.

The pilots validated both hypotheses, along with several other assumptions, including:

The customer and the Facebook teams are open to new ways of working. The Innovation Hacking framework allows Facebook teams to have a different kind of conversation with their clients. Rather than pitching products or selling specific outcomes, the sales teams listen to their customer's unique needs and challenges, and help them generate, prioritize, and implement ideas.

Innovation Hacking drives both short- and long-term outcomes. Innovation Hacking helps Facebook teams to have both tactical *and* strategic conversations with their customers, addressing both short- and long-term goals. This results not only in a robust pipeline of sales opportunities, but leads also to real, actionable outcomes. For example, one pilot customer shifted their entire Q4 strategy based on the experience, which opened a whole new line of investment for the sales team that sustained into the future. The team estimated that the experience could unlock an additional $3M in recurring revenue.

There is value in cross-functional collaboration. The Innovation Hacks bring together diverse stakeholders—marketing, communications, sales, strategy, finance, product, or sometimes even HR or manufacturing—from both the customer and the Facebook organization, as well as the customer's media agencies. Not only do these various perspectives contribute to a broader range of ideas; it also increases the likelihood that ideas are actually implemented due to the buy-in and alignment that is generated across teams and organizations.

The cross-functional nature of the program is a markedly different way of working for Facebook's customers. In fact, for some of them it was their first time working across the aisles. As a side effect, those engaged in the project elevated their political capital among their colleagues.

On Facebook's side, the cross-functional design allows the team to grow their influence and develop new contacts within the client organization, beyond their usual media and marketing collaborators. At the same time, involving Facebook team members beyond media signals their commitment to helping the client with their challenge. It is a win-win solution for everyone involved.

Continuous Improvement

Even after formally launching the program and engaging additional customers, the consulting team continued to iterate on their approach. Following each engagement, they collected feedback from both Facebook and

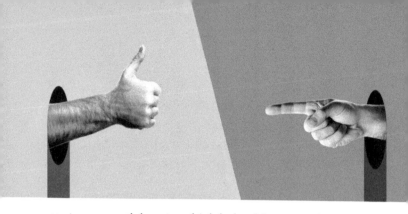

customer participants, which helped fine-tune the experience. This spirit of continuous improvement has kept the project nimble and responsive to key learnings, including those outlined below:

Make the investment worthwhile. Innovation Hacking requires a significant investment of resources from both the customer and Facebook stakeholders. During the pilots, it became quickly apparent that identifying the "right" customers with the "right" problems at the "right" time is critical to ensuring the best use of the required social capital.

The "right" clients are those with whom a sales team is looking to grow their relationships, influence their marketing strategy, and/or help them think beyond short term outcomes. Engaging a client's executive leaders or decision makers in the process was critical to the project's success, and the most successful Innovation Hacks have executive leaders attend the workshop, as well.

During the pilots, it became quickly apparent that identifying the "right" customers with the "right" problems at the "right" time is critical to ensuring the best use of the required social capital.

The "right" problems for Innovation Hacking

- Support the client's broader strategic and business goals,
- Allow for a pipeline of short-term and long-term possibilities,
- Are relevant to Facebook's expertise, strengths, and resources,
- Don't require a significant amount of research or specialized expertise outside of the core team, and
- Are issues that the client teams are passionate about.

Innovation Hacking Challenges the various companies faced differed significantly depending on the industry context:

- How might to maximize synergy among individual brands to increase the overall market share? (Consumer Product Goods)
- How to identify occasional guests and increase the frequency of their visits? (Food & Beverage:

- How to increase preference of the brand among the young AB audience? (Beauty)
- How to acquire 50 million new unique buyers by 2020? (E-commerce)
- How to improve brand perception beyond pricing, closeness & assortment? (Retail)

It became evident, that the "right" time to do an Innovation Hack is during moments when they can have the most impact on the clients' business (e.g., before major planning cycles, whenever there is a strategic shift in business priorities, or when a sales team wants to intentionally grow their client relationships).

Meeting clients where they're at

One of the differentiating elements of the Innovation Hacks is the *Consumer Insights Presentation* where the Facebook team shares market trends, consumer research, and/or external inspiration related to the client's challenge. The presentation is an excellent opportunity for the team to add value through new perspectives, demonstrate care, and position themselves more competitively. While this level of customer-centricity is a new muscle for most sales teams and tends to take the most time to prepare, it is a critical component of the process. By empathizing with the client's challenge and pain points, rather than pushing media solutions, the Facebook team can open the door to more strategic conversations with their clients.

Maintaining momentum

After the first few Innovation Hacks, it turned out that some clients are better at implementing the Action Phase than others. Some teams struggled to know how to help their clients prioritize the ideas that came out of the Innovation Hack. To respond to this challenge, the consultants designed a *Prioritization Meeting* at the end of the Innovation Hack workshop to assess each of the ideas based on their desirability, feasibility, and viability. This meeting has proven to be critical to aligning the next steps and moving ideas forward, especially if some of the initiatives require mid- or long-term implementation.

Impact and Scale

As the program evolved, so too have the metrics to track success. Initially, success was evaluated based on participants' feedback on their experience. Would they recommend it to others (net promoter scores)? Did they feel the workshops resulted in innovative ideas? Were they a valuable use of time? – etc. These metrics may be favorable indicators of success, but in order to scale, metrics also need to include business results.

So, in addition to sentiment, they began tracking financial and relationship metrics over time. How much new sales pipeline was generated (tracked through Facebook's CRM)?. What new lines of investment have emerged because of Innovation Hacking? How many new client contacts were created? The combination of both qualitative and quantitative metrics has helped the team make the case to scale the program to more clients across Latin America, delivering a total of 29 Innovation Hacks over the course of a year and a half.

While Facebook's clients – the world's largest brands – have had a remarkable experience, it has also resulted in material success for Facebook's business, generating a 20x ROI measured in sales pipeline generated by the initiative.

By leveraging the current trust in your own business network, it is possible to entice different stakeholders to achieve a common goal, as long it is genuinely based on addressing the main stakeholder's needs.

Enabling Innovation and Change

The experience that involved multiple organizations in multiple countries showed that collaborative approaches like the one described here are useful interventions that help teams increase revenue with clients or partners, broaden relationships and deepen trust, or drive innovation to solve common challenges.

By leveraging the current trust in your own business network, it is possible to entice different stakeholders to achieve a common goal, as long it is genuinely based on addressing the main stakeholder's needs, in this case Facebook's clients. It is what inspires and agglutinates the efforts.

Once the intention to serve the main stakeholder needs is clear, a well-designed program can guide multiple teams into building, sharing, and creating together. Inspired by design-thinking methodologies, the *Chal-*

They also discovered that by joining forces they could act as an enterprise team that added tremendous value as opposed to separate teams solving specific technical issues. Collaboratively pursuing this higher goal of solving the clients' strategic challenges was a change enabler that allowed many of them to experience doing the best work of their careers.

lenge Phase, the *Ideas Phase* and the *Action Phase* guided increasingly larger groups to accomplish specific tasks throughout the weeks, leading to the day in which all the stakeholders got together to create a common understanding of their business challenge and craft innovative solutions.

It was inspiring to see that, through the these practices, Facebook professionals changed their mindsets, and consequently changed their attitudes. They realized first-hand that they could leverage the trust they had built and positioned themselves differently, challenging the clients to act in new, more productive ways.

They also discovered that by joining forces they could act as an enterprise team that added tremendous value as opposed to separate teams solving specific technical issues. Collaboratively pursuing this higher goal of solving the clients' strategic challenges was a change enabler that allowed many of them to experience doing the best work of their careers.

It is possible to break silos and drive innovation with the intelligence already available within existing teams. It is possible to foster autonomy and empower people to step up to a higher game. It is possible to bring together a diverse set of stakeholders that would not normally collaborate and enable them to find innovative solutions to common challenges.

Maybe what is required is just to innovate innovation.

Agustín Couto empowers teams in global organizations to perform at their very best. He's currently director of Learning and Leadership Development at Pure Storage.

Kelsye Gould, M.S., is a Manager at The Design Gym where she helped develop and facilitate the Innovation Hacking program.

Gian Taralli is Director at ?What If! Innovation, part of Accenture

Jason Wisdom is a Co-Founder and Partner at The Design Gym. the global strategy and innovation consultancy behind Facebook's Innovation Hacking program.

www.thedesigngym.com

By Michael Nichols

Corporate Innovation: Quo Vadis?

Incubate and Accelerate Exploratory Innovation

Can corporates innovate? Should they? These questions haunt both corporate executives and academics practicing and studying corporate innovation. While the temptation is to respond with a resounding affirmation and even with a sense of duty to society, the answers to these two fundamental questions are not as clear as practitioners and theoreticians would like to believe.

Starting with the first question, it is not difficult to find examples of companies which have successfully innovated in their core business and beyond. The Ball

Corporation transformed from a producer of glass jars to a packaging and even an aerospace company. Amazon started as a web shop for books and has transformed into a dominant web and cloud services company. Some even predict it will become a dominant logistics company. Hilti changed its business model from a producer of tools to one that provides a tool-on-demand service.

One would not have to look far for an entire graveyard of corporates which failed to innovate and were either cast into the dustbin of history or have been drastically downsized from their former glory.

Such examples of successful business model innovation come readily to mind, but more often, the story resembles the infamous downfall of Kodak. One would not have to look far for an entire graveyard of corporates which failed to innovate and were either cast into the dustbin of history or have been drastically downsized from their former glory.

From the point of view of corporates hoping to sustain their success, the data seem to confirm that the situation is deteriorating, not improving. While the past is certainly no predictor of the future, the trend lines of chart 1 suggest that corporate lifespans are shrinking over time. Why? For one, the amount of capital needed to challenge incumbent business models is getting smaller and smaller. Startups which can demonstrate early traction have access to almost unlimited capital, and new technologies make the capital requirements needed to threaten incumbent players less burdensome. Another reason is that – also thanks to technology – the borders which used to delimit an established market vertical are either blurring or vanishing entirely.

Consider the automotive industry which for most of its history has had seemingly insurmountable barriers to entry. A startup would have to put up massive amounts of capital for hardware development, factories, warehouses, and logistics. All of that does not even include the necessary go-to-market capabilities, such as an established network of suppliers, strong branding, franchisees, and more. These entry barriers are fast eroding as the industry faces multiple existential threats from unpredictable angles.

For starters, software – a very different industry vertical – is increasingly dominating the game. Some may categorize Tesla even as a software company, given the company's software-defined-vehicle approach. This trend has forced the traditional automotive players to compete in a space which is not their home turf. The jury is out on whether they will be able to transform themselves, but successful business model innovation is rare, especially when the DNA of the company is hardware, not software, and the formerly protective barriers to entry have become a sort of self-imposed prison the incumbents have a hard time breaking out of.

Adding to this challenge, young customers seem to have begun moving away from an ownership model to a just-get-me-from-A-to-B model. Uber – yet again from another vertical – has forever changed how we all conceive of mobility. What happens to established automotive companies when drivers transition to riders, when they no longer care to own vehicles, when the only brands they care about are ride-share companies?

If corporates hope to survive, then they must innovate.

Should Corporates Innovate: Two Competing Ideologies

Before asking how corporates can best innovate, the fundamental question remains: Should they be the vehicle to do so?

Two competing schools of thought have emerged in this context. One follows the logic Clayton Christensen laid out so well in *The Innovator's Dilemma*. To summarize it crudely: corporates cannot innovate beyond their core business and should spin out any potentially disruptive business model. Why? Because corporates are exploitation engines. They know how to squeeze every bit of cash, efficiency, and productivity out of known business models or known systems. Every KPI, every structure, and even the culture itself has evolved to serve this purpose – but it only works for the current model. Once an organization deviates from the established model – so the theory – the probability of success plummets to near zero

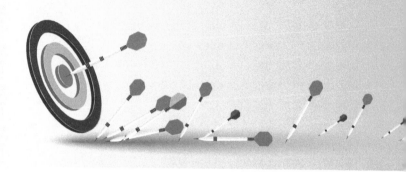

The second ideology does not deny Christensen's logic but argues that it is possible to exploit existing business models while exploring new ones – provided it is done carefully and with the right organizational setup. Success may be rare, but we know this so-called dual approach is possible because it has been done. This thinking is better known under the theory of the ambidextrous organization put forth by O'Reilly, Tushman, and others.

To summarize, one approach believes that disruptive innovation within corporations is essentially hopeless. Consequently, disruptive business models need to be spun out, and the focus lies on inorganic growth vehicles such as M&A or perhaps external venture builders. The other one claims that innovation is not hopeless, but very difficult, and it can work by leveraging core competences and focusing on internal venturing such as incubators and R&D.

The world is much grayer and messier than the theories. Innovation is a game of probabilities in which nobody can safely pick winners. The players must launch many unsuccessful shots to have a chance of scoring the winning goal.

However – as corporate innovators, do we have to choose between the two? Like with many ideologies, the world is much grayer and messier than the theories. Innovation is a game of probabilities in which nobody can safely pick winners. The players must launch many unsuccessful shots to have a chance of scoring the winning goal. As with many theories in social science, things depend on context and circumstances. So, why limit ourselves to only one set of vehicles? Let us try them all and see which shots on goal land in the net.

Inorganic or Organic Innovation – or Both?

Now, let us turn to the more practical question of how to approach corporate innovation. Here, the answer depends on the strategic growth gap, i.e. how much growth is wanted or needed. If a large company wants to increase its market share by 20% or more, it must grow by billions of dollars. In most cases, this cannot be done with business as usual, so the company must think about strategic innovation: which strategic arena to focus on, which customers to target, with which value propositions, which business models? Which capabilities to leverage, and – even more important – what not to do? Once these questions have been addressed, the company must decide which vehicles it will deploy to achieve its growth ambitions.

There are various options to consider when trying to fill the strategic growth gap, and each of them has its tradeoffs. All are fraught with high failure rates when it comes to innovating outside of the core business. Even M&A, often seen as a panacea, suffers from high integration failures of up to 80%. To reiterate the message from above, do not limit yourself artificially to one set of tools, but rather view them as a portfolio of tools which can be deployed to achieve the desired growth, each with its own risk profile and contribution to the growth.

I have been working for the last 9 years in corporate incubators, accelerators, and venture capital at both a large multi-business German corporate (Robert Bosch GmbH) and a more focused family-owned German SME (MANN+HUMMEL); it has allowed me to experience success factors and challenges in practice.

rganic growth/innovation

Type	Strengths	Weaknesses
Technological Advances (R&D)	▶ IP protected ▶ Create products based on deep customer knowledge and existing IP	▶ Expensive ▶ Slow ▶ Too tech-centric with insufficient business model validation ▶ Integration into business units very difficult if too exploratory
Internal Ventures (Incubation/ Acceleration)	▶ Create new business using existing talent and resources ▶ Talent attraction and identification ▶ Use existing advantage of core business (e.g. sales channels)	▶ Channels often inaccessible to venture teams ▶ Inappropriate governance applied by inexperienced executives (e.g. put profit targets before more qualitative metrics to measure traction) ▶ Integration into business units very difficult if too exploratory

Inorganic growth/innovation

Type	Strengths	Weaknesses
M&A	▶ Lower market risk since target has proven traction ▶ Avoid slow, expensive R&D ▶ Faster expansion	▶ High integration failure rates ▶ Misaligned cultures ▶ Pervasive overvaluation ▶ Insufficient value creation

Do not limit yourself artificially to one set of tools, but rather view them as a portfolio of tools which can be deployed to achieve the desired growth, each with its own risk profile and contribution to the growth.

ybrid growth/innovation

Type	Strengths	Weaknesses
Partnering	▷ Avoid expensive in-house development ▷ Focus on strength of organization	▷ Difficult to align internal and external partners with an appropriate incentives ▷ Slow negotiations ▷ Unclear ownership
External Ventures (Incubation/ Acceleration)	▷ Lower market risk ▷ Independent from existing business units ▷ Lighter, more appropriate venture governance ▷ Experienced entrepreneurs	▷ Unclear whether revenue or valuation is the target ▷ Unclear mandate in the eyes of shareholders (i.e. can invest their own money for better returns)
Corporate Venture Capital	▷ Lower market risk ▷ Test new business models without having to build them ▷ Market sensing ▷ Zero-cost business development	▷ Difficult to balance strategic impact and portfolio return ▷ Maturity mismatch between startups and core business units ▷ Long-term returns with small short-term impact

If companies are set up correctly to address these conflicts, incubators and accelerators offer huge untapped potential and the opportunity to build the capacity to innovate on innovation itself.

Corporate Accelerators and Incubators: The What

Incubators and accelerators are often used as synonyms, but they differ in the maturity level of the venture. An incubator typically focuses on very early-stage ventures which have an idea and need to validate its potential for a repeatable, scalable, and profitable business model by testing it with real customers using demos, MVPs, or other experiments. Based on the feedback they receive from the market, ventures may have to change directions multiple times or give up. The largest risk at this stage – and the top reason new ventures fail – is that new ventures are unable to find a sufficiently severe customer problem that makes customers change their behaviour and even pay for a solution.

Accelerators, on the other hand, focus on the stage after incubation in which ventures have found early traction and want to accelerate this traction by concentrating on early productization and creating a repeatable sales process. They also have high rates of failure due to the

difficulty of industrializing and going to market, challenges which are often underestimated.

Incubators and accelerators can be internal or external. Internal ones focus on building corporate ventures with corporate assets. External ones focus on providing programs for external startups, perhaps granting them access to internal resources. There are also hybrid models in which internal and external teams work together to validate their ventures.

Corporate Accelerators and Incubators: The Why

Incubators or accelerators will not close the entire strategic growth gap of a corporation. Nevertheless, they are an excellent vehicle for testing and de-risking new business models.

In theory, a company can leverage the comparative advantage it has amassed in its core business to explore new business models, which is nothing less than creating the foundation for the ambidextrous organization. In practice, ambidexterity runs into obstacles the moment a new venture should be integrated into the existing business. The reasons for this are manifold and well known: channel conflicts, conflicting financial KPIs, the perception of innovation as a cost, no well-defined strategy, no upfront commitment of resources.

However, if companies are set up correctly to address these conflicts, incubators and accelerators offer huge untapped potential and the opportunity to build the capacity to innovate on innovation itself.

Corporate Accelerators and Incubators: The How

To run an effective incubator or accelerator with a chance of producing winners, companies must have several critical pieces in place:

Strategic Innovation Theses

To run an effective incubator or accelerator, the strategic innovation theses must be documented and crystal clear, which includes laying out the growth goals, the search fields – or hunting zones as some call them,

*The probability of failure, which
is already astronomical for new
ventures, is almost certain if
governance or process are missing.*

acceptable business models, a theory for value which
might raise eyebrows, since innovation is supposed to
be about divergence. However, in practice, divergence
from the company strategy is certain death for an
innovation project. If you do not have a clear strategic
perspective, stop the project before you start, because
it will be a monumental waste of resources, talent,
and morale.

Upfront Resource and Capital Commitment

In line with a clear strategy, commit resources and
capital *upfront* in case one of the ventures successfully exits the program. Too often, budget allocation
depends on a successful exit. That's a mistake. While
it is prudent to make the release of budget to the
venture dependent on successful traction and exit by
stage, do not wait to allocate this budget to the portfolio holder who runs the incubator or accelerator. The
mechanism matters. Off-cycle budgeting is just as – if
not more – important than the methods and tools used
in the incubator or accelerator. Equally important, do

not attach budgets to single ventures, because that creates the perverse incentive to keep them alive even when there is no traction. Remember, failure rates are high, and throughput is critical. Make sure the budget sits at the portfolio level to foster better incentives for the entire funnel.

Strong Portfolio Governance and Innovation Process

At first glance, governance and process seem antithetical or even inimical to innovation. However, experience demonstrates that without them the probability of failure, which is already astronomical for new ventures, is almost certain if governance or process are missing. Why? Without portfolio governance, too much money is tied up in losing ventures which eat up all the cash that could be placed in other, more promising ventures. Running a

A true culture of innovation is built by doing innovation, treating it just as seriously as the core business, not by going through motions or creating the semblance of innovation.

portfolio requires dispassionately terminating ventures without traction or without fit. Failure to do leads to insufficient bets being placed to have a chance of producing the rare winners.

Accordingly, the corporation must have a strong process in place that ensures testing the right hypotheses at the right time in a capital-efficient manner. The stages a venture goes through are well known, and how much should be invested at each stage is equally well known. Corporates would do well to be as strict as venture capitalists are in their evaluation and tracking of startups.

Proper Organizational Structure, Sales Channel Alignment

Assuming a company has somehow managed to do all the above correctly, what happens if a venture eventually exits these programs successfully? Where does it go? Do you integrate it into the core? Do you set it up as an independent unit? Do you spin it out? Some have the temptation to say, 'wait and see.' While nobody can pick winners upfront or know exactly what the final business model may look like, the answers to these questions are crucial – so crucial that if you do not have an answer, you should not start the incubation or acceleration process.

Let's look at one of these options in more detail: – integrating into the core. While this seems to be the most obvious route, it might be the most difficult of all. If the venture was not planned for, budgets may not be available. If the venture is not mature enough for the KPIs of the core business, it will surely be killed within the core. If the venture's sales model differs even slightly, the established sales channels will either refuse to work with it or will not be properly incentivized. All that can mean certain death for a new venture. Therefore, it is imperative that the willingness and commitment to integrate the venture are aligned in advance, and this means dedicated budgets, headcount, sales channel incorporation and incentives.

A Final Remark:
Tear Down the Innovation Theatre

Many leaders mistake entrepreneurship for the festivities and rituals that accompany it – pitch events, hackathons, agile sprints, and more – believing that these events are good for culture building. But in reality they create only the pretense of innovation. Their actual effect is the demoralization of your talent once they figure out it was a show and nothing more. Worse, they may leave with your IP. A true culture of innovation is built by *doing* innovation, treating it just as seriously as the core business, not by going through motions or creating the semblance of innovation.

Conclusion

If I look at my innovation experience with a large multi-business corporation such as Bosch or at a smaller, more focused SME like MANN+HUMMEL, size does not make a significant difference. Success depends on how ingrained the core business is into the thinking, the KPIs, the culture, the processes, whether there is a willingness to experiment, and how innovation is perceived. Many see it purely as a function of technology development; I see it as foremost a social phenomenon. Ultimately, innovation is a people and leadership challenge.

I may have posed more questions than I have given answers, because the practice of innovating is subject to innovation itself. Try things, do not get stuck on one method or tool, and *act* – you cannot innovate unless you start.

Michael Nichols joined MANN+HUMMEL in 2022 where he is Director of Corporate Ventures. From 2014-2022 Michael worked at Bosch, where he was responsible for the Bosch Accelerator Program and for the implementation of a Bosch-wide innovation process.

 By Colin Mayer

Re-structuring Organizations for A Better World

O n December 20th, 2023, the Financial Times named Lars Fruergaard Jorgensen as its Person of the Year. Outside of a small group his is not a name that leaps immediately to many people's minds at the end of a turbulent year for the world. That itself speaks volumes for the qualities of a great leader.

Jorgensen is the CEO of a company that until recently was not exactly a household name either. Novo Nordisk is a Danish pharmaceutical company, still best known for the product on which it was founded a hundred years ago in 1923, insulin, which is used in the treatment of diabetes.

Jorgensen was appointed CEO in 2016, a traumatic year in which Novo Nordisk had to layoff 1000 people, its stock market value fell 15%, and it was subject to lawsuits from patients and the wrath of the newly elected President, Donald Trump, about price gorging in the USA.

By contrast, this year Novo Nordisk became the most valuable company by stock market capitalization of any company in Europe, just overtaking LVMH for the top spot, and the largest charitable foundation by assets in the world, the Novo Nordisk Foundation, with more than double the assets of the next largest foundation, the Bill and Melinda Gates Foundation.

Great leaders come and go, and today's corporate stars are tomorrow's fallen angels and bankrupt companies. So, one should not read too much into one person or one company's experience. Nevertheless, there is something about the context as well as the person that can be learnt from this example about leadership.

By way of context, it is worth understanding that Denmark, the home of Novo Nordisk, is currently one of the world's most successful countries. It has one of the highest levels of GDP per capita, lowest levels of inequality, best employee relations and happiest citizens of any country in the world. Again, like leaders and companies, great nations rise and fall, and the economic success of Denmark has depended to no insignificant extent on

Great national leadership does not necessarily come from politics or government alone, but also from business.

Novo Nordisk – by some accounts, Denmark would have fallen into recession over the past year had it not been for Novo Nordisk's contribution.

Enterprise Foundations

But here too there are lessons to be learnt, particularly that great national leadership does not necessarily come from politics or government alone, but also from business. To understand this, it is important to appreciate that by international standards both Novo Nordisk and Denmark are unusual. Their common distinctive feature is enterprise foundations. Novo Nordisk is an enterprise foundation and Denmark is home to the largest number of enterprise foundations in the world, with 40% of listed foundation enterprises being situated in Denmark.

What distinguishes enterprise foundations is, not only that they have a foundation, but that the foundation owns the companies. As in the case of Novo Nordisk, they are often listed on stock markets, but they have a foundation as a controlling shareholder. That is the basis of their success, the success of Jorgensen as a corporate leader and the success of the Danish economy.

The concept of an enterprise foundation is that the founder of a company should be able to preserve the purpose of company that they have established through a foundation that owns a controlling shareholding in the firm. Unlike other countries, Denmark has an enterprise foundation law that regulates the behaviour of such entities to ensure that they do not abuse their privileged status and uphold their founders' intentions. It lends stability to such companies, preserves their purposes, and promotes a long-term perspective.

Denmark has an enterprise foundation law that regulates the behaviour of such entities to ensure that they do not abuse their privileged status and uphold their founders' intentions. It lends stability to such companies, preserves their purposes, and promotes a long-term perspective.

Their leaders should be seen in this context because it means that what is being sought of them is to promote the long-term, philanthropic as well as commercial objectives of the foundation. It differs from the conventional stock corporation listed on stock markets with dispersed, predominantly institutional, shareholders who prioritize short-term financial performance. Even enlightened CEOs of such entities who believe corporate responsibility and sustainability is in the long-term interests of their shareholders frequently must battle against short-term financial pressures from hedge fund activists, hostile takeover bidders, and high frequency traders.

A combination of managerial
discretion and long-term stability
are preconditions to eliciting
the best of management.

Great leadership derives from as well as creates great
companies, and great companies come from supportive
institutional arrangements created by their founders.
Even in the US, where we attribute companies with traditional stock markets, it is often the institutional structure
created by the founder that is the basis of the most innovative firms. From Henry Ford, who had to experiment
with three different corporate forms before he found one
that granted him sufficient freedom from his investors
to develop the model T, to Larry Page and Sergei Brin,
who founded Google with a dual class share structure
that gave them voting control over the firm, it is ownership structures reviled by shareholders but demanded by
founders that sometimes perform the best.

A combination of managerial discretion and long-
term stability are preconditions to eliciting the best of
management. Lars Fruergaard Jorgensen is only the
fifth CEO in Novo Nordisk's 100-year history. Compare
that with a median tenure of around 5 years in the UK
and the USA and one can see the different horizons and

pressures under which CEOs operate in different corporate contexts.

There are several other features that distinguish inspiring leaders who can put their ideas into practice. The first is purpose – corporate purpose and the clarity with which that purpose is communicated. There is much evidence that companies with a strong sense of purpose outperform others financially as well as socially and environmentally. However, that depends on the clarity and precision with which the purpose is enunciated.

That points to two important aspects of leadership and that is communicating the company purpose and embedding it in the organization. Good leaders recognize their role as communicators-in-chief rather than commanders-in-chief. They bring their corporate purposes to life through narratives and examples that emphasize not just the success of the company in delivering on its purpose but the challenges and failures that it faces as well. That reflects the importance of authenticity and demonstrating that leaders not only walk the talk but also talk the truth. As an illustration, Lars Fruergaard Jorgensen was quite open on becoming CEO about the conflicting challenges he faced in addressing criticisms from consumers and politicians in the USA about Novo Nordisk's excessive pricing and from shareholders about its inadequate profitability.

It is those at the bottom who have the specific knowledge and understanding of the aspirations and problems of their customers, communities, and colleagues.

But there is another reason for demoting the commander-in-chief role of CEOs and that is CEOs should do for the rest of the organization precisely what the organization has done for them – namely empowered them. It is not only the board of directors that should have a real sense of ownership of the corporate purpose but so too should everyone in the firm, from the board to the shopfloor. Everyone must understand their part of the corporate purpose and how they can contribute to its fulfilment in exactly the way in which a janitor at NASA in 1962 responded to a question from President Kennedy about what he was doing with the words "Well, Mr President, I am helping to put a man on the moon".

Key to this is empowering people in the organization with the discretion to determine how they can contribute to the corporate purpose. That requires organizations to invert their traditional hierarchies and delegate authority from the top to the bottom. It is those at the bottom who have the specific knowledge and understanding of the aspirations and problems of their customers, communi-

ties, and colleagues. The board has the generic under-standing of the corporate, industry and economy wide issues that need to be addressed but not the specific individual, communal and local ones.

To address this, boards of firms must satisfy the finan-cial demands of their investors at the same time as the rest of the organization is meeting the needs and desires of their customers and communities. That requires placing trust in employees to promote the corporate purpose based on the companies' values and culture.

The research departments of pharmaceutical companies, particularly biotech ones, illustrate this very clearly. They are staffed by scientists who prize their independence and objectivity as much as academics. Attempts by senior management to impose their authority over their researchers can have damaging consequences for the willingness of the researchers to participate, as the Swiss pharmaceutical company Roche realized when it sought to consolidate the ownership and control of its biotech subsidiary Genentech in 2009. Assuring their researchers of the continuing independence of Genentech was essential for preserving the different values and culture of the biotech from the pharmaceutical parts of its business.

But it is not just culture and values that need to be aligned with the purpose of the business – so too do the hearts and minds of people who work in the organization. What distinguishes successful leaders is their ability to inspire their employees with a sense of the importance and significance of the work that they are doing. Just making money for others is not in itself inspirational but doing so on the back of a purpose of addressing major human, social or natural world challenges is.

Purpose Creates Opportunity

What Novo Nordisk has done over several years has been to discover what its real purpose is. It used to be simply to produce and sell insulin profitably. That is a description of what the company does, but it is not a purpose in the sense of the reason why a business is created, why it exists and its reason for being. How has the creation of the business changed the world and why would the world be worse off it didn't exist? This is a question about a meaningful challenge that the business exists to address and a significant problem that it seeks to solve for its customers, communities, and environment. But it must do so in a particular way because it is not a charity.

A business exists to solve problems that you and I face as individuals, societies and the natural world in a form that is commercially viable and profitable for its investors and shareholders. So, it is seeking to "produce profitable solutions for the problems of people and planet". Novo Nordisk has over the last few years come to appreciate that its purpose is not just to produce insulin profitably but to help people treat diabetes, which might involve taking insulin but often does not, and to avoid getting diabetes in the first place, which is influenced by lifestyles, especially diets.

Defeating diabetes through different forms of treatment and changes in lifestyles is a meaningful and inspiring challenge and purpose for those working in

A business exists to solve problems that you and I face as individuals, societies and the natural world in a form that is commercially viable and profitable for its investors and shareholders.

an organization. It also helps to address concerns about excessive pricing by promoting ways of addressing diabetes that do not necessarily involve taking insulin. In the process of doing this, Novo Nordisk not only helped address diabetes around the world, including in low- and middle-income countries where 80% of type 2 diabetes is found, but also transformed the firm from being the financially struggling one that Lars Fruergaard Jorgensen inherited into the most valuable company by stock market valuation in Europe today.

The reason for this is that in repurposing the company, it realized that a key aspect of both avoiding and treating diabetes was weight control. Nutrition is a critical factor and obesity a primary cause of obesity. Semaglutide is a treatment that works by reducing patients' appetite and therefore their consumption of food. In the process, it became recognized as not only a potential treatment for diabetes but also a weight reducing drug that is now marketed as such under the name Wegovy. The search for treatment for one medical condition – diabetes – led to the discovery of another related treatment for being overweight. This became a blockbuster which has led to Novo Nordisk's fourfold valuation increase since the middle of 2019.

With Purpose Comes Trust

Identifying the meaningfully challenging purpose of Novo Nordisk to defeat diabetes led to the discovery of a drug that has created a related but distinct market for the company. If Novo Nordisk had stuck purely to a profit driven objective it would have sought to have sold ever more insulin at ever higher profit margins by cutting costs and laying off still more workers. In the process it would have failed to have created, and indeed undermined, the most important and financially valuable asset which a company can possess – and that is to be trusted.

Trust lies at the heart of commercial activities. Trusted corporations are more commercially successful because they promote more loyal customers, more engaged employees, more reliable suppliers, and more supportive societies. But there is one further critical aspect of ensuring that companies build and retain the trust of their customers, employees, suppliers, and societies and that is that they should not only produce profitable solutions to problems, but they

should not profit from producing problems for others either. They should not profit from imposing expense on others. Instead, they should incur the costs themselves of avoiding causing detriment for others or where it occurs mitigating, rectifying, or remedying the harm that has been done.

Lars Fruergaard Jorgensen recognized straight away the damage that accusations of excess pricing were having on the company and its reputation, and he sought to address this while still preserving the profitability of the business. The relations that Novo Nordisk built with governments as well as businesses and not-for-profit organizations around the world in identifying alternative ways of treating and avoiding type 2 diabetes were critical to achieving this.

Companies build and retain the trust of their customers, employees, suppliers and societies by not only producing profitable solutions to problems but they should not profit from producing problems for others either.

Great leaders communicate not only the remarkable advantages and inspiration that derives from working for their profitable problem-solving not problem-creating businesses but also the meaningful partnerships that can be built with governments around the world. No business can on its own solve the world's major challenges. It must work with others and especially be trusted by government to promote, not undermine, the public interest.

That is what visionary founders create, what inspiring leaders promote and what great companies achieve.

__Colin Mayer__ is Emeritus Professor of Management Studies at the University of Oxford. He was the first professor at the Said Business School at Oxford, and Dean of the School. He led the British Academy programme on the Future of the Corporation and his book "Capitalism and Crises: How to Fix Them" has just been published by Oxford University Press.

By Marsha Ershaghi and
Maria Colacurcio

A Data-driven Approach to Workplace Equity

C ompanies are feeling the heat to achieve workplace equity. Employee demands for fairness,
shareholder pay equity proposals, the new
EU Equal Pay and Transparency Directive,
and expanding pay transparency legislation in the U.S.
are all ratcheting up the pressure for proof of progress.

However, while these collective forces contribute
to a general acceptance that workplace equity should
be prioritized, most companies are not effectively tying
efforts to the bottom line. As a recent report from Tapestry Networks and Syndio reveals[1], most organizations

---

1 https://synd.io/advancing-workplace-equity-from-the-boardroom/

lack the analytics to make a clear connection between investments in workplace equity and concrete business outcomes.

Boards are in a pivotal position to drive organizational commitment to workplace equity. However, the absence of metrics that show how workplace equity can deliver tangible impact for the business hinders boards from effectively overseeing it.

What does to take for companies to not only prioritize workplace equity but also link it to their overarching business objectives? How can they foster an environment where equity isn't just a buzzword but a fundamental driver of success?

Eliminating boards' blind spots

Board governance of workplace equity is driven by the urgent need to comply with changing legislation and get ahead of costly brand reputation issues. However, boards often struggle to ask the right questions about workplace equity and apply pressure to the executive team due to lacking the necessary data insights.

Most organizations' workplace equity programs lack clear targets, meaningful accountability, metrics, reporting structures, or effective integration with business objectives. According to our findings, 85% of HR and Total Rewards leaders and practitioners see room for

The new EU Equal Pay and Transparency Directive, and expanding pay transparency legislation in the U.S. are all ratcheting up the pressure for proof of workplace equity progress.

improvement in how well their organizations measure the success of workplace equity initiatives.

Boards should regularly ask to see key metrics that enable focused effort, and which drive action and accountability. One DE&I leader said, "You should be able to give that macro-level view on one page so the board understands where there's a problem, what's working, and where they can get insight."

Boards seeking a more informed approach are driving management to report with more granular detail around data, metrics, and benchmarking. For example, directors would like to see more information around representation in specific leadership roles and the roles that feed into those roles. They want to understand which talent has high potential, what is their career path and who are the people moving through different career paths. Boards are looking for more than a snapshot — they want to understand trends over time. They are also looking for benchmarking that compares their demographics to peer organizations to help them gauge the level of progress.

Below are questions boards can ask management about workplace equity initiatives:

- Does leadership have shared accountability and a common understanding around workplace equity goals and value in the organization?
- What workplace equity analyses—e.g. representation analyses, diversity benchmarking, promotion and attrition analyses, and pay equity and unadjusted pay gap analyses — is leadership conducting? How often? For which employee identity groups and intersections?
- How does leadership assess employee sentiment—are there disparities in how employees feel?
- How does leadership track progress toward workplace equity goals and ensure accountability and transparency? What benchmarks are they using for comparison?
- How is data disclosed? What is communicated to investors and other stakeholders?
- What is the right balance of transparency for communicating progress internally and publicly?

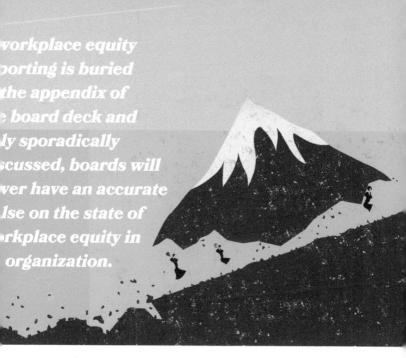

workplace equity reporting is buried the appendix of e board deck and ly sporadically scussed, boards will ver have an accurate lse on the state of rkplace equity in organization.

Key pillars for effective oversight

There are several foundational elements that collectively underpin a board's ability to oversee workplace equity, driving both its prominence and impact:

Structural integration into the board's agenda: How and where workplace equity shows up on the board agenda speaks volumes about an organization's commitment. Workforces are dynamic, so if workplace equity reporting is buried in the appendix of the board deck and only sporadically discussed, boards will never have an accurate pulse on the state of workplace equity in an organization. Rather, workplace equity reporting should be a consistent priority on the agenda on par with financial reporting.

Diverse board composition and leadership: Diversity of thought, experience, and values in a board's composition can influence vigilance around and exposure to workplace equity goals and value. An executive shared, "Through board diversification, DE&I became a part of the dialogue, and the transformation gave the CEO a platform to speak on this as a topic in board meetings. It's been a game changer."

The business case for equity: It's crucial for organizations to draw a clear connection from workplace equity to business outcomes, supported by data insights. Top leaders often speak vaguely of workplace equity as "good for business" but are at varying levels of maturity in how they link efforts to tangible business outcomes such as resilience, growth, innovation, and profitability. A director said, "We can't lose sight of the business aspect of this, because where a lot of companies fall short is that 'this is a nice thing to do' versus a business imperative that actually drives better results." The issue with vague reporting and ambiguous targets is that workplace equity often ends up perceived as cost rather than as drivers of business performance. Consequently, this results in workplace equity programs struggling for resources and attention.

A culture of accountability: According to HR analyst Josh Bersin, about 80% of companies are just going through the motions of equity and diversity, and are not holding themselves accountable. Using data to set and forecast realistic and specific targets is key to creating accountability. A director encouraged boards to treat DE&I targets like financial targets to hold management accountable. They said, "If [a DE&I goal] were a revenue target, you'd figure it out, right? You'd figure out how to get there because that's what you do — so figure this out."

Candid concerns from board directors

A recent discussion series with over 60 board directors and top Talent, HR, and Diversity executives revealed several notable concerns and areas of focus for advancing workplace equity:

Boards lack a shared language to define, investigate, and advance workplace equity. There is a wide lexicon of similar-but-different terms for workplace equity concepts, such as "pay equity", "pay gap", and "opportunity equity" that need to be demystified. By aligning on a unified vocabulary, boards and leaders can achieve greater clarity in moving towards measurement and informed action.

Analytics and data help boards drive more informed decisions and guidance. Boards are seeking frameworks for measuring workplace equity as there are no widely established standards to benchmark workplace equity progress or set diversity and equity goals and strategies. Hard data can empower HR leaders to analyze and report on all these critical aspects to their board. Transparency can drive action. Sharing data may not lead to sudden change but puts leadership on notice and can create space for change through awareness, opportunity, and mitigating unconscious bias. One director said, "When you have a governing framework around the metrics, you have better traction."

Connecting workplace equity priorities to tangible business objectives is important, but difficult. A director said "DE&I must be a business initiative with business value and business impact." This is especially important in a volatile economy, as all-too-often workplace equity is not a budget priority for many companies

"Leaders need to choose courage over preservation". Having access to data analytics to substantiate assertions and validate resource requests is a crucial element in empowering leaders.

There are now five generations in the workplace who have differing approaches to information exchange, communication, expectations around transparency, and collaboration.

that face economic, supply chain, and operations issues. To connect these dots, workplace equity programs must be rigorously measured so that efforts can be tied to business outcomes such as talent resilience, innovation, and risk mitigation.

Ever-expanding transparency requirements are bringing pay and opportunity issues out from behind closed doors. The EU Equal Pay and Transparency Directive is the new global high-water mark for pay transparency as it requires both pay scale transparency and public reporting on mean and median pay gaps. In the U.S., there continues to be a groundswell of state and municipal laws that require salary range transparency. As employees are given greater visibility to their peers' pay ranges, organizations are under increased pressure to explain pay and assure employees of pay equity. On top of that, new requirements in states like Colorado and Illinois, as well as in the EU Equal Pay and Transparency Directive, reflect an emerging trend for opportunity transparency around promotions and career growth. In this context, data analytics are critical to credibly respond to these requirements — and to future-proof organizations for emerging regulations and stakeholder demands.

Leaders must be empowered to make courageous and educated decisions. Board directors and management need to have the courage to say what needs to be said and not worry about not being elected to the board again or having the same role within a board. As one director put it, "Leaders need to choose courage over preservation". Having access to data analytics to substantiate assertions and validate resource requests is a crucial element in empowering leaders.

Boards can lead the way

There are now five generations in the workplace who have differing approaches to information exchange, communication, expectations around transparency, and collaboration. This demographic diversity continues to challenge the traditional models of the workforce structure. There are opportunities to learn from unique perspectives, foster mentorship, and create experiences that can only strengthen corporate culture and drive innovation.

To emerge successfully, they need to retain and promote their best people — without bias. Pay equity is foundational, but it's just the start.

After hundreds of conversations with boards and executives, these insights remain key:

Leaders need to listen more. Even during some of the most complex investigations or corporate breaches, employees just want to feel like they are valued, that there is equity, trust, and recognition. Talent equity and retention are linked to business resiliency. Company culture must start with accountable leadership that operationalizes trust and open communication.

Resilience is paramount. Today's businesses grapple with a turbulent economy, an ever-changing regulatory landscape, and widespread pressure from their employees. To emerge successfully, they need to retain and promote their best people — without bias. Pay equity is foundational, but it's just the start. The more employers can embed equity into their entire employee lifecycle, the more trust they'll build with their people, and the more enduring the business will be for the challenges and opportunities ahead.

Data is the key. Boards must push organizations to leverage analytics to benchmark where they stand, then set goals and pinpoint impact areas. With metrics to guide their decisions, boards can step up their oversight and ensure a workplace where every employee — and in turn, the business — thrives.

Marsha Ershaghi leads the governance practice at Tapestry Networks, a firm connecting board directors, executives, policy makers and other stakeholders to jointly tackle complex challenges.
www.tapestrynetworks.com

Maria Colacurcio is the CEO of Syndio, a research and advisory firm that provides technology and expert guidance for measuring, achieving, and sustaining all facets of workplace equity.
www.synd.io

By Bernie Jaworski and
Virginia Cheung

Book Overview

Creating the
Organization
of the Future

Building on Drucker and Confucian Foundations

Why Drucker and Confucian Foundations?

This book is based on Virginia's dissertation which focused on the comparison of Drucker and Confucian philosophies. Both thinkers were fundamentally concerned with a harmonious and functioning society. For Drucker the majority of his life's work was focused on a functioning society. And, since society transitioned from farming and local communities to a "society of organizations," Drucker felt that organizations needed to be well-managed for society to function well. At the time of Confucius, society was largely comprised of families in small, farm-based communities. For society to function well families need to function well. His viewpoint was that each individual needed live a life of based upon a moral foundations, in particular integrity, benevolence, kindness, and values. Thus, with different units of analysis (families vs. organizations) both thinkers had a strong point of view of what an effective human being (or leader in the case of Drucker) needed to embody and role model for society to function well. As such, we used their thinking as the foundation of our work.

Introduction

Our experience is that most organizations start with a product or service idea. In the case of a product, the engineers go to work to craft a better solution than exists in the marketplace. The aim is to provide a product that is regarded by the market as much better than competing offers. If successful, the product or service gets adopted by innovators and over time the organization gains customers, adds employees, and experiences revenue growth. If all goes well, it grows from a small start-up to a healthy mid-size or large firm.

At this stage, we observe that organizations take one of two paths. The first is positive. The firm continues to renew itself. It closely monitors marketplace developments and can meet current marketplace needs as well as transition to the future marketplace. Thus, it balances competing in two time periods, the current marketplace, and the future marketplace. This is what Peter Drucker termed "managing continuity and change" and it is the essence of Confucius teachings "the only constant is change itself." For a variety of reasons, this is very hard to do. Within the semi-conductor industry, we have examples such as AMD, Intel, Texas Instruments, and Nvidia.

The second pathway is quite the opposite. the firm "locks" in on a business model, optimizes the business model, and, as a result, is unable to reinvent itself to

Both Peter Drucker and
Confucius had a strong point
of view of what an effective
human being needed to embody
for society to function well.

compete in the future. S3 and Silicon Graphics are examples of firms that competed well in a particular historical period but were not able to pivot to a new business model. Unfortunately, many firms follow this second path. As Confucius noted "If the situation changes, I change too. Just like the shadow follows the shape of things." Drucker's constant admonishment was to abandon products, processes, and strategies that no longer "fit" the realities of the marketplace.

There are many reasons why this pivot does not happen. One critical reason is that the senior leadership remains technology- or product-focused rather than asking the basic question of "what business are we in?" Kodak was not in the business of cameras and film: It was in the business of creating memories. The technology to make memories is constantly evolving, but recording these events will ensure that they are with us forever. Back in the 90s, Texas Instruments was in the business of defense, personal computers, semi-conductors, calculators, and other initiatives. It would be difficult to address the question of "what business are we in? Today, they are laser focused on core enabling technologies (i.e., semi-conductors) that create the future.

Five Fundamental Direction-Setting Domains

If one is satisfied with just competing with a core product in one historical time period, then it may not be necessary to set a sustainable direction for the firm. However, if the organization aims to be around for a long period of time, it is essential to address five fundamental domains which we cover in our recent book, *Creating the Organization of the Future: Building on Drucker and Confucious Foundations*. They provide an overarching goal for the firm that transcends a particular historical period as well as the values and culture to achieve the target. In the best of all worlds, the direction-setting activities place the firm on a course not just to respond to marketplace developments but to shape the evolution of the market.

If we reflect on market leaders – Tesla, TSMC, Microsoft, and Apple – they also shaped the evolution of their markets – they did not simply 'respond' to marketplace

needs. They influenced the evolution of the "five forces" that impacted their industry structure. From this vantage point, industry structure is a variable to be managed rather than something that exists outside the boundaries of the firm. As Drucker often reminded us, great executives do not simply adapt to changing market conditions; rather, they influence the economic conditions in which the firm competes.

In particular, we are talking about five key areas firms need to focus on:

- **Mission.** The mission enables the firm to go beyond the "offering" to focus on the core customer benefit. The core customer benefit in Disney's case – storytelling – lasts for decades if not centuries. It is not bound to one historical period.

- **Vision.** The vision articulates the fundamental target or goal for the enterprise. What does the world look like when you have accomplished your mission? Often this vision takes decades to achieve: It is ambitious, motivating, and energizes the workforce.

- **Purpose.** The purpose of an organization answers a simple question, "why do we exist?" At the most fundamental level: how does your community or society benefit from the presence of your organization? Why do you make the world a better place? A strong purpose is rooted in ways that organizations help society function.

- **Values.** The values of the organization provide the guardrails for ideal behaviour in the firm. How are we going to go about achieving our mission and vision? What is the right set of beliefs and behaviours to guide all employees?

As Confucius noted "If the situation changes, I change too. Just like the shadow follows the shape of things."

- **Culture**. Culture is how the work currently gets done inside the firm. What are the rituals, norms, and beliefs that shape how work gets done now? What type of culture does the firm want to put in place to compete now and in the future?

The first three of these five domains are externally focused. The mission answers the question what business your organization is in, and the vision focuses on the achievement of that mission (i.e., what is the specific goal that we achieve if we accomplish our mission?). Both address your served market. Your purpose is also rooted in the marketplace, but it reaches beyond your immediate customer as it relates to the broader community and the societal impact of your mission and vision. The key question, "why do we exist?," must be answered from a societal perspective.

In sharp contrast, the remaining two domains of direction-setting – values and culture – focus on how the work gets done within the organization. What are the principles under which we want our organization to ideally operate (i.e., our values) and how can our culture support our vision? Different missions and visions require different cultures, so the setting of values and culture generally should come after establishing your mission, vision, and purpose. A mission that is focused on "convenience and easy access" requires a very different culture than one focused on "the best cutting-edge technology." The former may emphasize a customer-service-driven culture while a technology orientation may mean focusing on a culture of technology innovation.

The strategy of the firm must follow from setting the direction. Strategy – the specific, integrated set of choices related to "where to play" and "how do we win" in an industry – should be articulated in the context of a clear mission, vision, and purpose. Without that context, the senior leadership team has no rationale to make the important choices around which markets to serve (or not serve), the specific positioning of the organization, or the capabilities that must be built to support their position. However, we recognize that this is not an easy task. In a different context and era, Confucius noted in any significant journey "the way is long, but with every step one is making progress."

In the next section, we briefly review the central logic of our chapter on mission. If space permitted, we would have described all chapters. However, we chose mission since it is the starting point of most direction setting journeys.

A Closer Look at Mission

At first glance, well-crafted mission statements often seem rather obvious. However, our experience is that it often takes many months to answer the very basic question, 'What business are we in?' Peter Drucker stated the challenge as follows: *"Nothing may seem simpler or more obvious than to answer what a company's business is. A steel mill makes steel, a railroad runs trains to carry freight and passengers, an insurance company underwrites fire risks. Indeed, the question looks so simple that it is seldom raised, the answer seems so obvious it is seldom given. Actually, 'what is our business' is almost always a difficult question which can be answered only after hard thinking and study. The answer is usually anything but obvious."*

Equally important, the crafting of a mission statement is not simply a nice poster on the wall or a "who we are" message on the website; rather, it is one of the most important decisions of the leadership team. If the mission statement is narrowly focused on current products and technology, the firm will likely miss out on the next generation of products and technology. If it is too broad, it will not help focus the firm's resources – its R&D investments, its people investments, and its selection of target markets. Drucker believed that most firms did not give sufficient consideration to their business purpose and mission. He believed that this error was perhaps the *most significant* cause of business frustration and failure. There's similar advocation in Confucian teaching on the importance of setting a clear direction, he stated, "Noth-

In our experience it often takes many months to answer the very basic question, 'What business are we in?'

ing is as important as focusing upon the correct goal... when it is obvious that the goals cannot be reached, don't adjust the goals, adjust the action steps."

With these thoughts in mind, mission statements share six basic characteristics: (1) they focus on the core customer benefit, not the existing products or technology, (2) they specify their target customers, (3) they are short—often one sentence, and (4) must fit the theory of the business, (5) they inspire the workforce, and (6) every worker can see how their role can support the mission.

Focus on Underlying Benefits for Customers—Not Products or Technology

Mission statements are customer-centered. They answer the key question, "What is the core customer value that we provide to our target market?" They do not articulate current products, offerings, services, or solutions. Products are internally focused on what the firm does. Products change, but underlying customer benefits last years if not decades.

Specify the Target Customers

Mission statements must specify your target set of customers. For a company such as Microsoft the target market could be exceptionally broad and for a small startup the core segment could be very narrow. Indeed, one of the major problems with start-ups is that they often spread their resources too thin across many opportunities and segments.

Keep it Short—One or Two Sentences

Mark Twain once said, "I didn't have time to write you a short letter, so I wrote you a long one." In the same spirit, it takes a good amount of time for a senior leadership team to write a one-sentence mission statement.

Grounded in the Theory of the Business

Recall that a key component of Drucker's thinking is that the mission of the firm must fit the "realities" of the marketplace. He termed this ability to specify the core assumptions of the industry as a key part of his theory of the business. A mission statement must fit comfortably with the key trends, developments, and evolution of the industry. If the core profitability assumptions of the industry change (e.g., the profit in the industry shifts from the product itself to the services or information provided by the product), then the mission must be revisited.

Inspirational

As Drucker noted, a mission cannot be impersonal; it has to have deep meaning, be something you believe in—something you know is right. It is a fundamental leadership responsibility to make sure that everybody knows the mission, understands it, lives it. Drucker stated, "The mission is broad, even eternal, yet directs you to do the right things now and into the future so that everyone in the organization can say, "What I am doing contributes to the goal." So, it must be clear, and it must inspire. Every [stakeholder] should be able to see the mission and say, "Yes. This is something I want to be remembered for."

Every Employee Can Contribute to the Mission

Hence, each employee must ask the question, what can I do to support the mission of my organization? What strengths do I possess that enable me to direct my activities and results in support of the mission? This reflection on the "contribution of each individual to the mission" is a conversation each employee should have with his or her boss each year. This alignment with a broader collective purpose is consistent with Confucius' thinking that individual development is best focused on shared goals rather than individual goals. Similar to many other Eastern philosophies, Confucian teaching heavily promotes mutual responsibility and collectivism, and Drucker described Confucianism as an "ethic of interdependence, an ethic of mutual obligations." Indeed, if employees cannot see how their role can support the mission statement, the mission statement is not useful—and must be rewritten. Keep in mind: One purpose of the mission statement is to align all employees toward a common goal.

Building on Peter Drucker and Confucianism

In the title of our book we use the term "foundation" to emphasize that we are building on the work of Drucker and Confucius and moving it forward into the 21st century. In particular, we enhance and contemporize their work in five specific ways.

First, **business practices have advanced**. Today's business world is highly networked both in terms of "ecosystems" of players that compete against other ecosystems and in terms of the tidal wave of change brought about by digitization. Drucker could not have forecast these fundamental shifts. Furthermore, the emergence of purpose-led organizations and brands has only truly emerged since his death in 2005. Our key point is that the world of business has changed and that we need to update our thinking about this world to reflect this change.

Second, **business theory has advanced**. Much has been written in the past 20 years that has pushed our knowledge of management forward. For example, Drucker did not have a distinctive position on purpose. Rather, his writing on mission included purpose. Given how much has changed regarding the role of purpose in organizations--we offer the examples of Microsoft , J&J, Unilever, and several others as case studies in our recent book--we believe it is now exceptionally important to craft a stand-alone chapter on purpose. Purpose is distinct from mission, and this must be acknowledged. More generally, the advancement of business theory is reflected throughout our book.

Third, we have advanced our own thinking on the topic, and we want to share our perspective. For example, we specify criteria to assess the quality of the concept (e.g., five specific criteria to evaluate a mission statement). This is our perspective, not that of Drucker or Confucianism. We have spent a good deal of time thinking about these issues, and we want to share our viewpoint.

Fourth, **we shift from concepts to very practical guidance**. This is distinct from Drucker since he was focused more on the novel concept than the exact details of crafting the statements. This is not to say whether he would agree with us (or not), but "how to get started on the journey?" would not be part of a typical Drucker book or manuscript.

Fifth, **we introduce new concepts and language** to enhance the precision of work and reflect the changes that are unfolding in organizations. This is reflected throughout the entire book–in particular, the examples, criteria, and identification of the best-of-class illustrations in the first section. Each of these sections includes new thinking and language that moves practice forward.

The idea behind our book was to use the wonderful thinking of Drucker and Confucius as a platform for building practical and straightforward advice on how to construct your mission, vision, purpose, culture, and values--and ideally shape the markets in which you compete. We hope you enjoy the book and its timeless insights.

Jaworski, Bernard and Cheung, Virginia (2023), Creating the Organization of the Future – Building on Drucker and Confucius Foundations, Emerald Publishing Limited.

Bernie Jaworski is the Peter F. Drucker Chair in Management and Liberal Arts at the Drucker School of Management, Claremont Graduate University.

Virginia Cheung is an Associate Research Fellow at the School of Management, Shenzhen University.

By Alexander Mackenzie

The Art of Contemplation

A Storytelling perspective

*He who knows others is wise. He who knows
himself is enlightened.*
Lao Tsu

B y weaving artistic practice into leadership
training, executives can gain a profound understanding of organizational challenges and
opportunities, facilitating better decision-making. A well-told story appeals to intellectual intelligence
by presenting intricate information in a digestible and
relatable manner, fostering clearer strategic thinking
and visionary purpose.

Allow yourself to think differently about leadership
for a moment. Just imagine that the issue is not ***what*** you
know but instead ***how*** you know.

The Art of Contemplation

Contemplation in this context is the place where conceptual knowledge meets the non-conceptual. As a leader it is impossible to make sense of intellectual, emotional and visceral intelligence connections without resorting to the 'inward gaze' of contemplation.

Contemplation in this capacity has the scope to be qualitatively more engaging than thoughtful reflection. Contemplation opens the possibility of rising above the two-sided understanding of right and wrong and instead allows the compassionate response of 'perhaps'. Leadership that facilitates 'perhaps' is more rounded and open to creativity.

As Rumi, the 13-Century poet, puts it in his poem 'Story Water' when he says:

"Water, stories, the body,
all the things we do, are mediums
that hide and show what's hidden."

Instead of the fluency of concepts that are available to contemporary thinking, we can explore the alternative intelligence of visceral awareness. Visceral awareness has at its heart the field of contemplation. Contemplation knows what is 'on' before reasoning words.

Visceral awareness results in how the body feels with seminal fuller knowing. To be sensitive to how the body responds, is a decision to be viscerally intelligent.

A well-told story appeals to intellectual intelligence by presenting intricate information in a digestible and relatable manner, fostering clearer strategic thinking and visionary purpose.

If you are wondering about visceral intelligence, consider first the ancient art of mandalas and the use of images before words. They have a very practical methodology that underpins leadership. It has a visual appearance first, that later emerges as conceptual thinking.

Mandalas

Mandalas are images that act as visual metaphors of self-realization and group awareness. Although mandalas have their roots in eastern culture, they are pertinent today as prompts of awareness to throw a light on current business leadership practice. A mandala (Sanskrit for "circle") is an artistic representation of higher thought and deeper meaning. Mandalas have been used to explore the spiritual, emotional, or psychological work and to focus one's attention on what lives most saliently behind the surface.

As a leader it is impossible to make sense of intellectual, emotional and visceral intelligence connections without resorting to the 'inward gaze' of contemplation.

The details of the meaning of a given mandala depend on the individual or peers creating or observing the image, but mandalas in many cultures serve, more or less, the same purpose of centring an individual or community on a given narrative in order to encourage introspection and, ultimately, an awareness of one's place and purpose in the world; this awareness then allows for peace of mind.

Below is an example of a management group that decided to explore personal mandalas as a way to express themselves individually as a precursor to talking about how they felt being in the organization.

The creation of a personal mandala is used to explore and posit a reframing of the individual self and relevant organization mores. As such leaders are able to communicate and share complex concepts succinctly and coherently in a creative way. Through the proactive application of the spoken word and the active use of imagery in synchronicity it is possible to converse in a much more profound way, the individual's expression and personal understanding of leadership experientially.

What image comes up when you are asked to capture your essence as an image? How is this image influenced by peers contributing to this image? Before waxing lyrical about your potential as an informed ISTJ-type, or as a mover-and-shaker, you may find yourself talking about yourself as a type of tree or a style of boat, as an animal or vibrancy of colour, that has pictorially emerged in your image as a leader reframed.

A mandala image adds another layer of meaning to the more familiar use of post-it notes to explore personal sharing, which too often offers a more limited range of expression.

Organizational reframe

Organizational reframe is a more contemporary exploration of mandalas. A word-based exercise which results in the image above, can become more personal in feedback as one becomes more individualistic in response. Especially as you allow yourself to wax lyrical and use image words and metaphors.

Using written metaphors for actual lived experience and including a few words or a sentence about your-

Although mandalas have their roots in eastern culture, they are pertinent today as prompts of awareness to throw a light on current business leadership practice.

self and your peers, might relate to an actual experience within the organization, such as a 'cloudy sky' or 'walking a tightrope' or maybe the presence of a 'dragon' in your team. This process can quite inadvertently, without difficulty expose the participant, making them vulnerable as it creates greater awareness of the organizational underbelly.

The nature of metaphors and images, like poetry, have a natural tendency to being truthful and personal. Poetry is the language of the heart before it becomes the content of the head. Poetry is the domain of picture-building before it arrives at conceptual meaning.

The 'Big Picture' of Leadership

To work with the 'Big Picture' of leadership you will need to have a working knowledge of the 'little pictures' that often govern organizational life. It is important for a leader to become more aware of *how* they say what they say.

A group of senior managers from a corporate university create a shared image as an organizational reframe. Such an experience affords a sharing that is not possible with words alone. It illuminates contemplation to use color and image.

Your ability to 'see' the Big Picture of the organization determines your ability to lead in that organization.

Storytelling can also be an organizational reframe

Think for a moment about your living story. As a spoken personal narrative, it is a far cry from the fairy-tale narrative of Rumplestiltskin or the pictorial come-uppance that becomes evident in the Three Pigs. These stories are by design more like fables with a single point

of learning. They are not built to share the complexities of personal narrative. When we speak out loud about our personal anxieties and triumphs, we evoke compassion and understanding in the listeners.

It is also very different from the media saturation of 'alternative facts' and spin. The aim of such hyperbole is to enjoin a certain kind of prescribed attention rather than explore the truth. Such stories do not anticipate a search for a deeper human context. When we talk about the 'community' of the business and rather than leveraging personal praise as a relevant signpost for such a community, refer instead to the most significant KPI, we are at risk of not being perceived as trustworthy.

The story of the Odyssey may well be the first story ever written, but it has lessons today for the organization of the future. The questions are as timely today as they were relevant then. Questions such as:

- Whom do you trust as a friend in the organization?
- Who has got your back at work? Who do you support, whatever?
- What do you do, when you don't know what to do?
- What do the shadows out of sight conceal?
- What does bravery look like in this organization?
- When does a leader lead the way?

At the very least, learning to speak out a version of the Odyssey as corporate professionals can lead to laughter, telling a good yarn and taking a risk while sounding authentic and credible. The Odyssey is a rollicking tale of love and loss, of daring to do the unusual, of being driven by fame and treasure, of learning about real trust when the chips are down.

Rather, working with the enlightening aspect of story-making calls upon three types of intelligence:

- **The intellectual:** The ability of the leader to rationalize, use logic effectively, know the difference between fact and fiction, apply critical thinking to reduce abstraction and 'spin', are all important to demonstrate intellectual prowess in leadership.
- **The emotional:** The ability of leaders to relate to others, using their emotional intelligence to demonstrate prosody (the patterns of stress and intonation in a language), people awareness and seeing when character types are behaving true to form.
- **The visceral:** is most telling when leaders say nothing and instead rely on their presence and leadership persona to act out leading the way. This calls upon an attitude of contemplation that sits at the hub of leadership intelligence.

Storytelling relies on this Wheel of Intelligence.

In this frame of mind we can explore the story of the Odyssey, as one of the first ever spoken stories of all times, to ask the questions that have always faced a leader:

- When do you lead and how do you listen?
- How might deeper listening seem like a 'giving away' of control?

*It is important for a leader to become
more aware of how they say what they say.*

Another story, The Parzival Legend (the medieval
chivalric romance) asks us to discuss the context today
of the real difference between the fool and the hero in his
escapades to becoming a leader of all those around him?
It is worth contemplating for example how might it be a
deliberate business manner to appear gauche or naive?

When we combine these with artistic expressions
such as the mandalas about the self and reframes about
the organization, we may find ourselves with more questions than answers.

As the discussion moves away from academic certi-
tude to the challenge of leadership being a very personal
endeavor making calls on our integrity all along the journey, it can be a real time adventure!

It is our job to make sense of all this and luckily we
have intellectual frameworks to do this, as well as peers
that can be relied on as friends and, hopefully, a refresh-
ing sense of self-appraisal and wonder.

But it also helps no end, to have a practice of contemplation for our leadership. If we are unlucky enough to
work with someone who not only does not have a practice but who looks furrowed when anybody mentions
storytelling, image making or artistic thinking, we know
what it is like to *not* have a leader.

The Odyssey and the Island of the Lotus Eaters
This image is a depiction of one Urilicus, one of the heroes of the Odyssey who succumbed to the excesses of distraction in his quest for wealth until he was pulled away by Odysseus who dared to open his eyes to the temptation of pleasure.

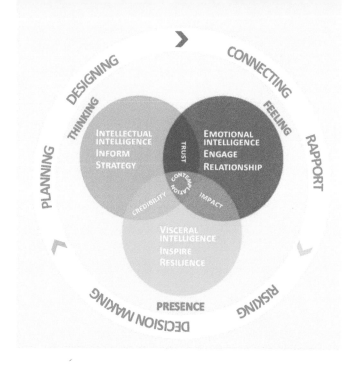

When we can embrace uncertainty, difficult decisions and meet unruly behaviour with joyful abundance, you can be sure that a leader in the organization is not far away. If you are lucky enough to have a fearless leader, chocks away!

Contemplation is in the essence of 'Big Picture' of leadership

Big Picture leadership requires a form of contemplation that is a sophisticated use of the different kinds of intelligence that make up the Wheel of Intelligence. They

Storytelling cultivates empathy by sharing personal experiences and emotions, enabling leaders to connect compassionately with their teams.

are intellectual, emotional and visceral intelligence. Contemplation is the separate axis on which these three intelligences revolve.

Visceral intelligence uses the body and non-conceptual thinking as the center of self-awareness. Emotional intelligence holds others to account. Intellectual knowledge remains constant as the information is common to all.

Contemplation requires the user to put to one side that what has taken years to get right. It factors in conceptual thinking as only one dimension of understanding.

It respectfully asks the age old question "What do you do when you do not know what to do?"

Instead of an errant nonsense reply, this question asks from a well-trodden koan perspective. That is, the Zen Buddhist story-type that provokes great doubt, leading to greater insight, often in the form of a paradoxical anecdote or riddle without a solution.

It is the remit of the Art of Contemplation and its concomitant Big Picture leadership.

It asks us to be wise, trusting of the heart and to take risks. It also may ask us to be fearless.

Head, Heart and Body

Emotional intelligence is recognized as being crucial in building strong relationships and fostering teamwork. Storytelling cultivates empathy by sharing personal experiences and emotions, enabling leaders to connect compassionately with their teams. This in turn fosters trust, loyalty, and a sense of belonging among team members, with the end-game of leading to a more positive work culture.

Visceral intelligence, as the bridge that connects bodily feeling to what we intellectually know is sometimes overlooked and is crucial to the important role in making experiences impactful. Storytelling can engage the senses, and makes for establishing a lasting impression. Leaders who master the verbal art of crafting the spoken word, by being more aware of their prosody, and presence as well as being strong in visually reframing concepts, can evoke emotions better and influence and inspire their teams, driving them by example to achieve exceptional results.

The Next Step

It's time to take the next step. You can use your head and trust the difference between the Enneagram[1] or developmental models to factor a reliable way forward. You can

---

1 https://www.truity.com/test/enneagram-personality-test

use the Johari Window[2] or explore the merits of competencies as your organizational matrix.

You can rely on your team for the strengths of a Belbin 'Mover and Shaker[3]' to make a commercial difference. You can know that an optimistic choleric[4] has a different future plan from you and the more even strategic phlegmatic may take a broader view. This is the team that will shape the future of your organization.

It is you that is a measurement for confidence beyond words, that exudes your leadership style in your self deprecating laughter as well as being able to see the problem from both sides. It is only you that upholds your time out and your ability to contemplate the Bigger Picture and fashion the next chapter.

Alexander Mackenzie is an artist and an executive coach. His work lives on the intersection between creative initiative and corporate development. He has for many years led a storytelling skills program at Cranfield School of Management called Winning Hearts and Minds (WHAM).

---

2 https://www.gartner.com/en/human-resources/glossary/johari-window

3 https://www.belbin.com/about/belbin-team-roles

4 https://fourtemperaments.com/15-temperament-blends/

By Ingrid Pope

De-cluttering

Creating space for sustainability

"Hello, I haven't seen you for a long time. How are things?"

"Yes, it's been a while! Things are really busy. It's somehow even busier than before, though that hardly seems possible."

Does this sound familiar? I hear it a lot, from many leaders. Repeatedly. We seem to be at capacity, or probably somewhere beyond capacity, most of the time. And somehow from one year to the next, our busy-ness still ramps up. It has been an on-going trend for at least a decade and it is not slowing down. Quite the opposite.

Increased digitization of everything means that we have to carry out many more tasks than we used to: every activity now requires us to log onto an app or platform to go and do something ourselves.

Businesses are under incredible pressure to perform and deliver profits, especially in the current economic climate. Over the years, budgets have been whittled down again and again, leaving staff to deliver increasingly more with ever-reducing resources (both financial and human), more and more quickly. And this in an age where our life admin is also becoming increasingly complex.

The term "shadow work" was coined to describe all the tasks that we now have to perform as businesses and public services push more and more activities onto employees/service users. The joys of the DIY economy! The increased digitization of everything means that we have to carry out many more tasks than we used to: every activity now requires us to log onto an app or platform to go and do something ourselves, both at work and at home. Is anybody actually on top of all their passwords?

Taken individually, none of these activities are very difficult or time-consuming. But collectively, they add up to an incredible amount of time and mental energy to simply run the admin of our work and lives. We are at saturation, often spinning dozens of plates at once, and a small hiccup can make them all come crashing down. And that is before we even look at what we might need to deliver as part of our actual job.

This takes its toll. Burn-out and mental ill-health are on a steady rise, costing businesses dearly. The estimate in early 2023 was that work-related stress and burnout is currently costing the UK economy £28bn a year. For employees, the cost is not only their mental health, but also their physical health, their relationships, the ripple effects on their family and friends.

In this context, it can feel impossible to have the head space to consider the bigger themes of our lives. How do we focus on our vision (at work or at home), when our time and energy is spent fire-fighting every day and simply keeping going without falling off the treadmill?

How do we create the space to introduce an agenda as complex as sustainability in a way that it becomes the heart of everything that we do, rather than just another box that needs to be ticked?

Those are big questions that can feel overwhelming, and a typical reaction to big questions like these is

to retreat into the familiar and just keep going on our treadmill. And that is what I am interested in. I am curious about how the clutter in our lives gets in our way, in the way of the big stuff, and keeps us right where we are. Only once we actually see it all laid out, how it is interconnected, what habits we have developed and what choices are available to us, only then can we consider ways of de-cluttering some of that stuff that keeps us stuck where we are.

Clutter? What does that mean? And how does it have anything to do with driving a sustainability agenda as a leader?

How about your employees, how much mental clutter are they carrying these days and how much mental capacity do they have for change of any kind?

We go through life accumulating all manner of stuff. Some of that will be physical stuff. That is the obvious, tangible and most visible manifestation of this accumulation. But alongside all the stuff we can see is also stuff that is less visible: there are our thoughts, our habits, our inner chatter, our feelings, our emotions, our beliefs... Then, there is also the broader context and the organizational stories and beliefs, habits and assumptions...

In my work studying clutter and its effects on people and businesses, I identified a number of different types of clutter. Each type impacts on us differently, but they are all interconnected and together, they contribute to making us feel stressed and overwhelmed. We will take a look at a few of these types of clutter shortly.

But before we get stuck in a bit more detail, I do want to make one thing clear though. Clutter in itself is not a bad thing, far from it! Who would we be without our inner world of thoughts, feelings and emotions, or the items that make up our ideal work environments or our homely cozy spaces? And many of our habits that we have developed over our lifetime are very useful to us.

Alongside the number of hours in the day, the other finite resource we have is our mental capacity.

Clutter does need our attention, however, when it gets in our way, when it stops us or those around us from doing the big stuff, both at work and at home. That is when we need to take a closer look and step into action.

Now let's turn our focus back to our sustainability agenda. What types of clutter could get in your way from delivering the changes needed at the pace required? If you observe your patterns and habits around this topic, what do you notice? Let's take a look at what might trip us up.

The first and probably most obvious area to look at is our diaries, and that of our team(s). The likelihood is that most of our hours are already filled one way or another. We are busy, the world is busy, work is busy. So if we want to start doing something new (like thinking sustainably), we need to stop doing something else, at least for a while.

But so often, we are asked to deliver ever more, without the recognition that something else will have to give. Does this sound familiar?

Just like budgets running out, our personal resources are also limited and will become depleted. So of course we might look at what drains us versus what energizes us, and plan to build in those activities that will nourish us. But in the end, there are only so many hours in the day, and only so much that we can achieve. Unless sustainability is given sufficient time in calendars, it will not happen. How much time are you ring-fencing to focus on this in your organization and team, and is it enough?

Alongside the number of hours in the day, the other finite resource we have is our mental capacity. As increasingly more media stories report on all manner of topics related to climate change, the health of the planet, large-scale migration, rising inequality, the dying of the oceans, micro-plastic pollution and a host of other big macro-problems, what do you notice is your mental chatter around these stories? Do you give them much air-time in your mind? Is your brain at capacity with everything else you are dealing with at the moment? Or does it all feel too overwhelming to consider without falling into despair?

And how about your employees, how much mental clutter are they carrying these days and how much mental capacity do they have for change of any kind?

Our resources are finite. Just like there are only so many hours in the day, we also have only a finite amount of brain processing power in our pre-frontal cortex.

The pre-frontal cortex is located at the front of the

brain, and it is the part of the brain which carries out the executive function, meaning that this is the part of the brain where all our day-time processing takes place. It is where we take in information and make decisions based on goals, preferences, judgments on whether something is good or bad, where we work out consequences of our actions. This is essentially the machine-room that allows us to function, and which drives our actions.

And this part of the brain, this pre-frontal cortex, can only handle so many processes at any one time. Even if it is quite impressive in its abilities, it is none-theless limited, resetting itself and cleansing its memory whilst we sleep (so yes, looking at what clutter might get in the way of us getting a good night's sleep is also useful).

In our age of information overload, stimulus overload, out-of-control inboxes, addiction-inducing distracting communication and social media platforms – our digital clutter – as well as a general sense of never quite being on top of things, simply dealing with our day-to-day lives creates so much mental noise that makes it difficult to stay focused on any one activity or task for any length of time.

To implement anything new requires energy, we cannot keep piling change upon change and objective after objective and expect individuals to perform well if we do not first de-clutter and create some space for this new stuff. And so it is also for any sustainability agenda.

We need to clear some mental clutter to create head space for the thinking around the change that needs to happen to truly embed sustainability. Are you, your team

Our emotions are a part of us and we carry them with us in everything that we do. They are what makes us human, and in the age of the rise of AI, we might want to hold onto those as much as possible!

and the rest of the organization in a place where you are able to do this properly? What unhelpful mental clutter will you put aside in order to make this a success?

Finally, another area of clutter that gets in the way of us focusing on and implementing our sustainability agenda is our emotional clutter. Our emotions are a part of us and we carry them with us in everything that we do. They are what makes us human, and in the age of the rise of AI, we might want to hold onto those as much as possible!

So let's identify what emotions we might be holding around sustainability and consider how we might put them to good use.

Quite often when I speak with leaders, they seem conflicted and uncertain about what they feel. On some level, there is the above-mentioned despair and over-whelm, but on another level, there is also optimism and hope. The key is to find a way to hold all these different emotions simultaneously, simply acknowledging that they are there and know that they will be fluid. The same will hold true for everyone else around us too, and unless we pay attention to what others will feel at a particular point in time, we will fail to connect with and engage them as well as we might.

Yes, it might feel awkward to start talking about our emotions at work. But equally, if we cannot align our emotions with whatever we are trying to do, we will not be as successful as we could be, and it will all feel like an incredible struggle. So find a way to talk to your team about emotions, yours and theirs, about the topic of sustainability, and you might be surprised at what you find out.

We have now covered a few different types of clutter (in our diaries, in our minds, digital, our emotions – there are more!), and highlighted some that might get in our way. What do we do about it all?

Step 1: We call the clutter out for what it is. We pay attention to all the stuff that holds us back, keeps us stuck in what we have always done, keeps us safe from the unknown and from the difficult balance between doing what is right for the business as well as for the planet. We carry out an honest audit of how our personal and organizational clutter creates barriers to the delivery of our green agenda, and we identify what is required to overcome them.

Step 2: Once we know what clutter is in our way, we put together a plan of how we de-clutter some of this stuff. As with all good plans, we make this one as clear, measurable and achievable as possible.

Step 3: We get started on delivering the plan. Right now. Of course, we might get derailed as other business imperatives creep up and take over. But we return to our plan and continue to carry out our tasks one after the other.

Sound too easy? Everything does not always have to be hard because we expect it to be. The key is to step back and create some thinking time to hatch the right plan, as well as using all the talent around us because we do not have to come up with everything ourselves.

So what will you do today to create space for sustainability in your diary, mind and heart?

Because if you don't, who will?

Ingrid Pope is the de-cluttering expert. She brings clarity to the situation when the noise makes it difficult to see or think.

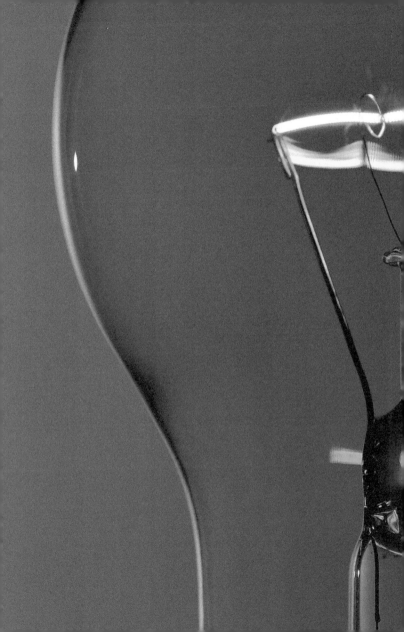

IDEAS FOR LEADERS

Academic research in accessible and engaging bite-sized chunks

IDEA #843

THE RISK OF IGNORING THE LESSER RISK IN PROJECTS

KEY CONCEPT

Most business projects or activities involve "conjunctive risk": they are successful only if multiple components are successfully executed. Decision makers often place too much emphasis on the riskier components of the project and neglect the less risky components—which could ultimately cause the failure of the project.

IDEA SUMMARY

Business projects, opportunities, or endeavours typically involve conjunctive risk—that is, the endeavour will succeed only if multiple, uncertain events occur. If just one of these required events fail to occur, the endeavour fails. For example, the success of a new product might depend on new technology and successful marketing. A technologically amazing product for which there is no viable marketing demand will ultimately fail. Conversely, the greatest marketing for a poorly made or functioning product will also ultimately fail.

To successfully manage conjunctive risk, decision makers must choose how to allocate their time, effort, or money—between, for example, technology development and marketing initiatives in the case of the new product described above.

According to a team of NYU and Dartmouth researchers, decision makers managing conjunctive risk often misallocate their resources. The core problem, according to their research, is how these decision makers respond psychologically to the likelihood of the multiple required events occurring.

The researchers created a series of conjunctive risk experiments in which the conjunctive risk involved one required event that was less likely to occur, which they called the weaker-link, and one required event more likely to occur, called the stronger-link. Without fail, the participants in the experiments engaged in a "worst-first" strategy, choosing to invest their time and effort in improving the chances of the weaker-links, while ignoring the stronger-links.

In the first experiment, for example, participants were given eight opportunities to win money if, in each case, two requirements were met—a stronger-link requirement that had 40% chance of success and a weaker-link requirement that had 20% chance of success. The overall chance of the participants winning the money was thus 8% (40% x 20%). In four of the opportunities, participants had the option of improving the stronger-link chance of success by 10% (from 40% to 50%). To do so required some effort: typing "ab" 45 times. They could not touch the weaker-link. In the other four chances, had the option of improving the weaker-link chance of success by 5% (from 20% to 25%), while the stronger-link remained the same.

Because the proportion of the improvement percentage was identical (i.e., 5% of 20% is the same as 10% of 40%), the participants' overall chances of winning the money increased the same whether they improved the weaker-links or stronger-links. Nevertheless, participants were more likely to expend the effort to improve the weaker-links chances of success while passing on improving the stronger-links chances.

In a second experiment, the figures were manipulated so that improving the chances of the stronger-link occurring had a greater impact than focusing on the weaker-link. A third experiment made the math explicit—that is, participants were given the calculations demonstrating that improving weaker-links was not necessarily advantageous. Yet another experiment involved reducing the chances of success because of theoretical budget cuts. In another experiment, the weaker- and stronger-links were described non-numerically (as two teams working on a hypothetical project, one of which was less likely to succeed, while the other more likely to succeed).

No matter how the conjunctive risk was presented or how the details might be changed, the majority of participants in all these experiments chose time and again to focus on the weaker-links and ignore the stronger-links. Psychology explains the results of these experiments, according to the researchers. When managing conjunctive risk, decision makers intuitively perceive the weaker-link as negative and the stronger-link as more positive. Because of what psychologists call the negativity bias, which over-emphasizes the impact of negative events, decision-makers intuitively consider these "negative" weaker-links as the more severe barrier to the success of their endeavour, and thus in need of investment—even if, in fact, improving the likelihood of a stronger-link occurring can have more impact on the overall chances of success for the project.

BUSINESS APPLICATION

Conjunctive risk exists in most business projects and endeavours. It is likely that success depends on the successful execution of multiple, independent components. This research indicates that decision makers may be too quick to focus their efforts and investment on improving the riskier components and undervalue the opportunities and benefits of improving the less-severe risks. It's possible that they will thus work hard to overcome one hurdle, only to then run into another hurdle that could possibly have been avoided.

This research also reveals the potential inconsistent expectations between top decision makers who decide which projects to start and project managers charged with implementing the projects. Firm leaders may discover that unexpectedly, project managers are over-investing in weaker-links and neglecting other critical elements of the project.

Leaders will want to ensure that slower, rational thinking rather than faster, intuitive thinking is guiding conjunctive risk decisions in their organizations:

REFERENCES
The Worst-First Heuristic: How Decision Makers Manage Conjunctive Risk. Joshua Lewis, Daniel Feiler, Ron Adner. Management Science (June 2016).

Access this and more Ideas at ideasforleaders.com

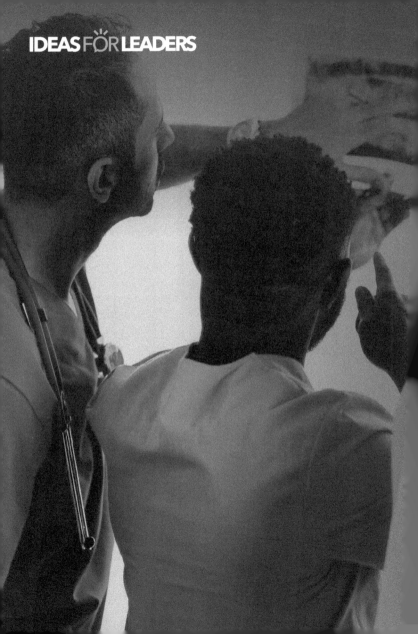

SPREAD INNOVATION THROUGH SHARED LEADERSHIP

KEY CONCEPT

A new real-world study traces how shared leadership among managers and professionals can ensure that innovation diffuses more widely.

IDEA SUMMARY

'Innovation can flourish in specific sections or units of an organization or system, but then fail to diffuse more widely. Two University of Warwick professors, Graeme Currie and Dimitrios Spyridonidis, studied the diffusion of 12 promising health care innovations from a citywide R&D unit to hospitals throughout the city. (The city is unnamed in the research.) The English National Health Service (NHS) tasked the R&D unit, called Metro Health-care Innovation (MHI), to initiate and diffuse health care innovations into everyday practice.

The results of MHI's innovation diffusion efforts were mixed: one of the innovations was adopted by only 3 other hospitals; other innovations would be adopted by 4, 6, 9, or 12 other hospitals; in one particularly success-ful diffusion, the innovation was adopted by 15 other hospitals.

The least successful diffusion occurred with a mental health innovation project (introducing a new community clinic aimed at improving access to mental health). The most successful diffusion involved chronic obstructive pulmonary disease (COPD), for which MHI introduced a new pathway to improve the safe discharge of patients, and improved the patient experience.

Through four years of extensive interviews, observations of meetings and review of official documentation, the researchers observed and analysed the evolving shared leadership dynamics of the 12 diffusion efforts — focusing especially on the COPD innovation to understand how leaders involved with the innovation were able to diffuse it so widely.

With most health care initiatives, three categories of leaders are involved:

- **Doctors**, who because of their expertise and knowledge tend to be the most powerful leaders in the system.
- **Nurses**, subordinate to doctors and whose leadership influence is more limited to other nurses only — influence that is based on hierarchy.
- **Managers**, who attempt to exert leadership influence over doctors and nurses through various mechanisms, such as human resource management and performance management systems as well as their involvement in organizational strategy, business plans, etc.

In the diffusion of innovation, how does shared leadership among these three categories of leaders evolve? In previous research on innovation leadership, managers are often given an outsized role over professionals (here, the doctors and nurses). In a health care setting, however, doctors, as mentioned above, have the greatest influence.

Conducted over the last four years of MHI's program, this research revealed that managers are indeed the more important drivers of innovation diffusion, but only in the early part of the effort. Then the doctors take the lead through their professional influence.

Specifically, the study showed that in successful innovation diffusion occurred in three phases:

Phase 1 (year 1-2 of the study): Managers created the climate for innovation through their initial mandate from NHS; seeking and providing resources from commissions; and implementing educational programmes related to the innovation to get buy-in from hospital chief executives and doctors.

Phase 2 (year 3 of the study): Doctors then took the lead as they facilitated the diffusion of the innovations into other hospitals by promoting the innovations to the city commissioners (thus influencing funding) and presenting the evidence to and educating their peers in other hospitals. Doctors in other hospitals also took a leadership role as they began adapting the innovations to better fit the situation in their hospitals.

While nurses followed the lead of the doctors, they also helped to adapt the innovations to local conditions, and provided valuable help in engaging frontline personnel.

Phase 3 (year 4 of the study): The doctors, still in the lead, focused on building medical networks to diffuse evidence and best practices related to the COPD innovation. Managers sought to provide resources to sustain the innovation but in general ceded leadership to the doctors, and nurses increased their leadership role in the adaptation of the innovation and engagement of nurses and other support staff in their hospitals.

The COPD innovation diffusion was a resounding success of shared leadership as all three types of leaders played their roles diligently. The researchers note, however, that some other factors beyond shared leadership also played a role in the varying success of the other initiatives, including financial challenges, disengaged nursing corps and less collaborative cultures, the latter which is key to the success of shared leadership.

BUSINESS APPLICATION

As revealed in this study, shared leadership among managers and professionals is different from hierarchical leadership in three ways:

- The "who" of leadership: hierarchical leadership is not about the personal attributes and characteristics of senior leaders; shared leadership involves practices enacted by leaders at all levels, although the top leadership role may evolve (e.g., from managers to doctors).

- The "what" of leadership: rather than top-down control and command, shared leadership takes place through social interactions among all levels of leaders; followers have a role to play in influencing and creating leadership.
- The "how" of leadership: shared leadership works through the skills and abilities of leaders to enable and enhance collective learning. Educating others — commissioners, chief executives, and doctors and nurses in other hospitals – on the merits of the COPD innovation was key.

Innovators trying to diffuse innovations throughout their organization or beyond should look for the leaders with influence who are willing to take on non-hierarchical, multi-level and evolving shared leadership roles in the process.

REFERENCES
Sharing Leadership for Diffusion of Innovation in Professionalized Settings. Graeme Currie & Dimitrios Spyridonidis. Human Relations (October 2018).

Access this and more Ideas at ideasforleaders.com

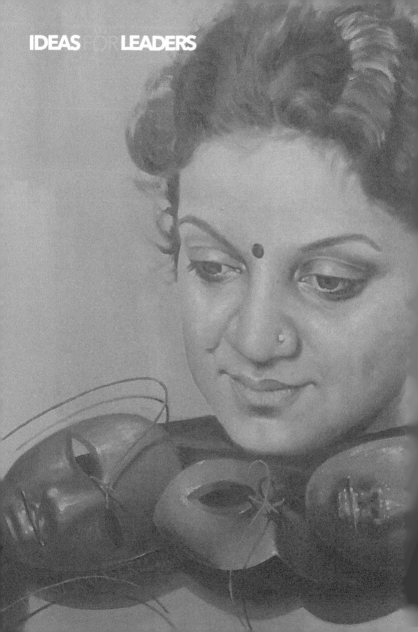

INTEGRATING SOCIAL IDENTITIES SPURS CREATIVITY AND INNOVATION

KEY CONCEPT

Psychological bricolage enables people to combine knowledge from their different social identities to enhance their creativity and find innovative solutions.

IDEA SUMMARY

Research has shown that creativity and innovation come from combining seemingly unrelated or irrelevant knowledge. You can create the context for combining unrelated knowledge by bringing together people with diverse backgrounds and knowledge. Thus, diversity (which might be based on race or gender but also on profession or function) is often sought in brainstorming teams.

However, unrelated knowledge also exists within individuals. Bringing together unrelated knowledge is what University of Michigan professors Jeffrey Sanchez-Burks and Fiona Lee, along with Matthew Karlesky of Suffolk University, call 'psychological bricolage.' The term bricolage refers to cobbling together different pieces to make something new.

For example, when typewriters still ruled the office, secretary Betty Nesmith Graham found a way to overcome the challenge of typos: she used her experience as an amateur artist to create a fast drying paint that could be brushed over the error and typed over (the new product was marketed as 'liquid paper').

Graham's breakthrough was made possible because Graham combined knowledge from two of her social identities. Social identities are the social groups by which we define ourselves or to which we belong, such as groups related to our race, gender, religion, profession, community, or organization. Different social identities — being a manager and being a parent, for example — are tied to different sets of experiences and knowledge. Graham was a secretary, but she was also an amateur artist. Drawing from both of these social identities allowed her to develop her creative solution.

However, replicating Graham's feat — which involves accessing the knowledge and experience from disparate social identities — is not as easy as it sounds.

The principal problem relates to the context in which social identities are accessed. You might, for example, access your professional social identity in the office, your parent social identity at home, and your football fan social identity at the stadium or during a match on television.

The issue of context is tied to the difference between insider and outsider social identities. For example, in a corporate strategy meeting, your social identity as a manager is an insider social identity (shared with the other managers at the table and relevant to the context of the meeting). Social identities tied to such things as being a volleyball player or a woman or a mom are outsider social identities, which are irrelevant to the meeting.

Graham's success emerged when at the office she combined her insider social identity (secretary) and her outsider social identity (artist). Many people, however, prefer to compartmentalize or separate their social identities, pushing the knowledge and experiences of outsider social identities to the background — especially when the insider and outsider social identities are seen as conflicting, such as being a woman in a male-dominated industry. Many people, in sum, are reticent about engaging in psychological bricolage, despite proof that incorporating the knowledge and skills from outsider social identities could enhance their creativity and innovation.

However, other people, echoing Graham's attitude, do not see their insider and outsider identities as incompatible, and are therefore less reticent about activating outsider identities. In psychological terms, such people are said to have 'high Identity Integration or high II.' People who feel their social identities are in conflict and prefer to keep them separate are said to have 'low II.'

Which brings us to this observation: Had Betty Nesmith Graham had low II, who knows how many wads of angrily crumpled paper would have ended up in 20th century office wastebaskets, until the personal computer came to the rescue.

BUSINESS APPLICATION

Given the creativity benefit of outsider social identities, organizations must take proactive steps to encourage psychological bricolage, especially from low II individuals. One method is modelled by Google's requirement for engineers to spend 20% of their time on personal projects — literally forcing them to put their insider social identities on the shelf. Even just asking employees to talk or think about outsider identities can make them more salient (i.e., relevant) to the workplace.

Studies show that external cues can be surprisingly effective in breaking down psychological barriers to outsider identity integration. For example, allowing people to work outside the office or even simply allowing casual wear at the office can help activate outsider identities.

Ironically, simply 'exposing' people to outsider identities — for instance, training people outside the organization for them to learn best practices from another company — can be counterproductive. Since your employees don't identify with the other company's practices, such attempts can only reinforce the differences between insiders and outsiders (between the way 'they' do things, and the way 'we' do things).

One final complication may be deciding which outsider identity to integrate into an office environment. The best answer: don't ask. Bring them all in. In psychological terms, this type of all-social-identities-welcomed attitude is known as general Identity Identification. People high in general II are the aces of psychological bricolage.

REFERENCES

Psychological Bricolage: Integrating Social Identities to Produce Creative Solutions. Jeffrey Sanchez-Burks, Matthew J. Karlesky & Fiona Lee. The Oxford Handbook of Creativity, Innovation, and Entrepreneurship (May 13, 2015).

Access this and *more Ideas at* ideasforleaders.com

The Daily Reset

365 Days of Wellbeing

By Steven P MacGregor

Published January 2024, ISBN: 978-8409565443

Dr. Steven MacGregor is a wellbeing pioneer and leadership development expert. He was an elite athlete in his youth, a national Duathlon champion, which he disarmingly describes as 'triathlon for bad swimmers', which brought him to the marginal gain training of cyclists and runners and then to the world of executive performance and well-being. Today, with over 20 years of experience in wellbeing and positive leadership, he is an advisor for McKinsey & Company and has worked with dozens of the world's leading organizations, as well as being an Honorary Professor on Health and Wellbeing at the Glasgow School of Art.

He is the author of a two previous books in the wellbeing space: Sustaining Executive Performance and Chief Wellbeing Officer as well as hosting the Chief Wellbeing Officer podcast.

Burnout. A word that was largely unknown prior to the 1960s, and is today part of common discourse. As we fret about AI taking over our jobs – and everything else – we should pause to consider that technology has so far only added to our work, increased the velocity of our working lives and submerged us in more data to analyse and digest than we ever thought possible, even two decades ago.

As such we are seeing talented managers and executives burning-out ever more regularly – and ever younger. Amy Bradley and Katherine Semler's book Running On Empty (reviewed in DLQ41) explored what organizations can do about this – but it is as much a duty of us as individuals to embrace our wellbeing and take action to combat the creeping effects of stress, lack of exercise and poor diet that accrue from forever having too many things on your 'to do' list, and failing to take the positive action to combat them.

The Daily Reset is Steven MacGregor's antidote to this. While the authors of most business books have high-hopes that their books will be read cover-to-cover but little expectation that they will be returned to on a regular basis, The Daily Reset is the opposite of that. It is specifically designed to be, in MacGregor's words 'engaged with' – dip in to it, go back to it, scribble notes and thoughts in it and experiment with the content.

There are 366 nudges, hacks, stories all designed to improve your behaviour 'to help keep wellbeing and a positive working life top of mind each day of the year' (there is even one for 29th February). Each is a piece of distilled wisdom, and prompts the reader to ponder a while or reflect differently on something – and hopefully to take action and engage with that idea.

While the book is a page-a-day through the year, it is also chunked into themes by month: Only 29 'Habits' for February but the full 31 for Movement, Sleep, Mindfulness, Exercise, Purpose, Resilience and Community.

The entries are pleasingly short – so you can absorb them quickly; and are hugely variable as the themes require. February 15th:

Exponential Gain: 1% better every day for a year: $1.01365 = 37.87\%$. 1% worse every day for a year: $0.99365 = 0.03\%$ This is the compound interest of small but consistent effort.

Most others are longer but not alot. June 24th

Go for a Good Gut: Bacteria make up 13% of all biomass on earth. (To put that in perspective, all the mammals on earth make up only 5%). Every one of us has between 300 and 500 different species of bacteria in our gut.... we need to keep these bacteria happy. It's important to promote good bacteria over bad. This is microbial health. You do this through prebiotics and probiotics: Prebiotics feed your existing bacteria...

Every book is a window into the author's soul in some way, and this book reveals plenty of MacGregor's life story in the reflections and choices of pieces he selects – which adds to the personal energy and passion he channels so effectively.

This is an updated edition of the book. The first edition was published in the midst of the pandemic and was clearly angled at a 'moving on from lockdown' type of wellbeing – this edition has done itself moved on from lockdown, and is a broader and more upbeat perspective on attaining and maintaining wellbeing through the slings and arrows of our daily lives.

As such it is a compendium of focused wisdom on well-being. There are a plethora of books selling bitesize wisdom out there, but The Daily Reset manages to differentiate itself from them, with that clear objective about striving for the goal of year-round wellbeing, and structuring itself in a way that allows the reader to apply the insights in that consistent, cumulative manner – all wrapped in the author's gentle yet emphatic enthusiasm and knowledge.

The Daily Reset is to be recommended to be used on a constant and consistent basis – but it is also will serve us well, even if we cannot do that, to dip into it and feast on the digestible delights it contains sporadically.

Certifiable

How Business
Operationalize
Responsible Sourcing

By Chris van Bergen

*Published: August 2023,
ISBN: 978-1119-890294*

News that Apple is making payments to iPhone customers, as part of a $500 million settlement resulting from the 'batterygate' scandal, should be a wake-up call for businesses everywhere.

At a time when sustainability is a watchword for business, built-in obsolesce really has no place. But lapses in corporate responsibility come in many forms. As with the Nike soccer ball scandal, one recurring source of trouble is the supply chain. Business leaders under pressure to find competitive edge while avoiding scandal walk a fine line, and managing complicated global supply chains can be where they trip up.

The key to ensuring a clean reputation, while still delivering on the bottom line, is the maintenance of effective responsible sourcing practices across the firm's supply chain.

In his new book, Certifiable: How Business Operationalize Responsible Sourcing, Chris van Bergen, a professor at NYU Stern School of Business, discusses how to create, implement, and audit sourcing practices that are not only environmentally sustainable and socially responsible but offer enhanced competitive advantage.

The book is not a vague call for an ESG Utopia. Rather it is a precise look at the dynamics of global procurement and sourcing and at the practical processes and systems required to transform an organization and its supply chain to be consistently responsible across all its operations. Central to Van Bergen's approach is a focus on transparency. Managers cannot possibly have eyes and ears everywhere but creating systems of standard setting and auditing that increase transparency across the supply chain, builds trust, and is the way managers can best keep tabs on maybe hundreds of suppliers and producers around the world.

Framing his welcome focus on practical solutions, Van Bergen provides valuable historical context, taking us through the evolution that led to today's thinking about supply chain transparency and responsible sourcing. He describes several corporate sourcing disasters where brands lost control over sub-contacting or relied on poor local regulation rather than creating and enforcing their own systems. While unfettered globalization might be seen to be the cause of these calamities, during the same time there were companies, described here, that instituted innovative policies that ensured good ethical practice.

Looking to the future, the book considers where corporate sourcing strategies are headed now that the world has become so much more aware of its social and environmental responsibilities, and corporate stakeholders more aware of reputational damage. With developments such as near-sourcing now being facilitated by technology and efforts towards a circular economy coming good, there are reasons to be optimistic. Yet in an era of extraordinary technological change—where workers can be replaced by machines—and at a time of alarming climate change, it is essential that business leaders and supply chain managers remain vigilant.

Van Bergen writes not only from the perspective of a business school professor and supply chain expert, but also as COO and CFO of Nest Inc., a global nonprofit working with the artisan and handworker economy to offer a service to the wider business community. "Nest's programs are bringing radical transparency, data-driven development, and fair market access to a fragmented industry, enabling handwork's unmet potential to improve our world." As with Nest this book, although based on altruistic theory, is fundamentally about practical implementation.

Higher Ground

How Business Can
Do The Right Thing In
A Turbulent World

By Alison Taylor

Published: February 2024, ISBN:
978-1-647-8234-36, 280 pages

lison Taylor is a clinical professor at NYU Stern School of Business and the Executive Director at Ethical Systems, a research collaboration of prominent business school professors working on ethical culture, founded by social psychologist Jonathan Haidt. She has spent over two decades advising large multinationals on risk, corruption, sustainability and organizational culture.

As the author notes in her introduction: 'It is easy to say companies should register a positive impact and help societies flourish, or listen to stakeholders to balance their interests. The devil lurks in how.' At the same time it is a need that requires to be actioned – and business executives who have been successful in their careers and have reached the top of the hierarchy, have most likely not done so with the skillset that is now required. Today's complex, inter-connected world of societal challenges and ecosystems requires something new.

While most executives are familiar with Adam Smith's Wealth of Nations and the ideas of competitive advantage, far fewer know of, let alone have read his first great work *The Theory of Moral Sentiments*. Business decision-makers are more expert on economics than moral philosophy as a rule. We know how to read a balance sheet when it is tracking dollars, but mechanisms to measure ethics and societal benefits are much less clear.

This road is strewn with contradictions and dilemmas, as Taylor observes 'companies are expected to balance conflicting stakeholder interests and demands: to follow clear global principles while adapting to local conditions and cultures; to solve societal problems while maintaining shareholder value; and to be transparent and authentic, with no empty talk or inconsistencies.' It is easy to understand that when faced with these competing demands executives opt for following the money, which is how the system is still predominantly structured and they are rewarded. It takes a special kinds of altruist to do otherwise – and they are rarely found at the peak decision-making positions.

The author is a business school professor however – and as such is tasked with finding a pragmatic, and teachable, route forward through this morass of complexity and contradictions. It is also worth reminding ourselves that all corporate titans are also humans, most with children of their own who frequently will challenge them – they have conduits to societal reality, even if the corporate world is good at making them difficult to access at work.

Taylor is realistic and pragmatic. "corporate responsibility' and 'sustainability' often describe corporate efforts to offset prior damage wrought by core business models by offering sunny, distracting narratives.... corporations must cater to a powerful appetite for accountability... [which means] that corporations must be more candid and realistic about problems they suggest they can take on.' At the same time she admonishes the habit of manipulating and undermining legal, political and regulatory institutions to serve corporate interests.

The first part of the book describes how we got here and what tools currently exist to deal with these situations. Part two is where the new thinking begins. New thinking in a fairly ancient sense, for we are talking here about ethics and human behaviour and the themes needing to be practiced could also have been found on the Temple at Delphi – such as gaining trust by practicing humility and curiosity.

Strategy is only the start, the real graft comes in managing the culture and your people, setting the conditions for change and adopting new mindsets.

Taylor is more granular when it comes to setting priorities; she presciently identifies that there will always be more to do, if you set sail towards being the most sustainable organization in the globe you will never be able to focus on anything else. It is important to identify the sustainable priorities that are core to your identity and mission as an organization – assess what is relevant with a materiality assessment.

Other areas she tackles with similar detail are tackling corruption, corporate political responsibility and managing transparency without losing credibility.

Part three – and this is why we like this book – Taylor acknowledges that strategy is only the start, the real graft comes in managing the culture and your people, setting the conditions for change and adopting new mindsets. In the conclusion she illustrates this with a case from BP and an employee who was disillusioned post-Deepwater, left, challenged the leadership and then returned when invited to lead their 'purpose' initiative.

Ultimately this is a book about culture. How organizations will only change in a meaningful, enduring way – and be able to reap the benefits of that – if the senior leadership creates the conditions for change to happen. No-one will make long-term, socially beneficial decisions in an organization if they know that they are, after the fancy talk and greenwash window-dressing is removed, only ever judged on a single line in the balance sheet: profit.

It starts with top leaders, but it needs to be woven through the whole business at every level. It's not that every employee should be able to recite the sustainable values of the corporation, it is that they should feel them; they should know that 'doing the right thing' in the book's subtitle, is the right thing to do for the business, the investors, the community they operate in – and for themselves.

Higher Ground is another clarion call for business leaders to enable their organizations to operate in a different way. Taylor expertly sets out the challenges and the practices they will encounter and need to adopt. It should be read by everyone who aspires 'to do the right thing' in their organization.

Power to the Middle

Why Manager Hold the Keys to the Future of Work

By Bill Schaninger, Bryan Hancock, Emily Field

Published: July 2023, ISBN:

978-1647824853

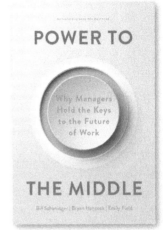

The authors, until recently, were all partners at McKinsey & Co, based in various offices across the USA. Bill Schaninger was a senior partner at the company, until October 2023. He advises on strengthening business performance through enhanced culture, values, and talent. Bryan Hancock is the global leader of McKinsey's talent work and sits on the board of their People Insights solution. Emily Field joined McKinsey in 2017 where she focuses on preparing leaders to manage the workforce of the future. All, unsurprisingly, base their work and advice on data-driven metrics.

Middle management is often seen as, if not a derogatory term, then certainly not an aspirational one. They have also over the years attracted a number of epithets that cast middle-management in a poor light: the clay layer, the innovation graveyard and so on.

But the reality is that middle managers are the engine of most organizations – and tellingly, often the employees that senior executives are most fearful of losing. Frontline staff can be replaced reasonably easily and there are always plenty of folk looking to rise into the ranks of senior executives, but middle managers are frequently more valuable in terms of their organizational knowledge and memories; they keep the wheels turning when things go wrong, and they are of course the indispensable link that takes senior executive strategy and translates it into real activity on the ground. They make sure stuff gets done.

However, the stereotype persists. Middle managers are too often disregarded, under-resourced in terms of development and have to play a careful game between those they lead and those they report to.

Today's reality is that organizations are much more dispersed, complex and forever evolving, and the need for capability in this middle level is more important than ever before.

Right from the start the authors' recognize these attributes stating 'that the smartest executives will do everything in their power to keep their best middle managers where they and reward them' and then explaining that in

The reality is that middle managers are the engine of most organizations – and tellingly, often the employees that senior executives are most fearful of losing.

many instances this is infact the correct approach, but it needs to be carefully managed.

Too often people are promoted out of roles they enjoy and excel at, into larger strategic and political roles, that they have neither real aptitude or wish to pursue, beyond the allure of a larger salary and the prestige of the next rung's job title. This does the neither the organization nor the employee any favours. The clever manoeuvre is to expand the middle manager's role, allowing it to incorporate more responsibility. 'When managers shed their roles as administrators and bureaucrats and emerge as true people leaders, their positions become invaluable and invulnerable to displacement'.

The McKinsey data the authors base this upon shows that nearly 75% of middle manager time is spent on tasks other than managing their teams; 39% on bureaucracy, 28% on individual contributor work leaving less and less time to do their core task – managing people.

The solution is to change the conditions, and create

a more attractive environment for middle managers to operate in. The book having described the problem goes on to set out their formula for enabling this to happen. The clue to what this is, lies in the title of the book – Power to the Middle. These are some of the key elements:

- *Rebundle jobs* rather than eliminate them. As workplaces transform with greater automation and AI, only middle managers have the granular knowledge and the wider perspective to reconfigure roles so that humans can do what humans can do best, and machines can do the rest.
- *Actively recruit and retain workers*. In a competitive job market, we know that people famously 'join organizations, but leave managers' – if managers are given more responsibility to recruit and retain their staff and outline the value proposition those roles will occupy, then there will be more purpose for both leader and follower.
- *Strive to connect the work to the people rather than the people to the work*. Managers are going to be ever more central to aligning individual purpose and corporate purpose – and designing solutions that show empathy while furthering the organizational goals.

If we can delegate authority and responsibility more wisely and more widely, then it gives purpose and meaning to those who are gaining it.

At the heart of this book is the simple proposition – one we see being promoted in many different guises from similarly experienced authors – of 'share the power'. Organizations invest huge amounts of time and money in recruiting 'the best' candidates for roles, and then when they have worked successfully over a period of time, often do not expand those roles to increase in breadth with the experience and capability.

If we can delegate authority and responsibility more wisely and more widely, then it gives purpose and meaning to those who are gaining it – and it unburdens others having to carry those tasks. The authors highlight tales of CEOs of large organizations still signing-off on recruiting managers three levels below them. By giving away authority on these tasks, senior leaders build their teams strengths and create more space for themselves.

A more powerful middle is, as your personal trainer will tell you, about core strength and greater resilience – it works for organizations as well as the torso!

About the Publishers

Ideas for Leaders

Ideas for Leaders summarizes the thinking of
the foremost researchers and experts on leadership and management
practice from the world's top business schools and management
research institutions. With these concise and easily readable 'Ideas'
you can quickly and easily inform yourself and your colleagues about
the latest insights into management best practice.

The research-based Ideas are supported by a growing series of
podcasts with influential thinkers, CEOs, and other leading leadership
and management experts from large organizations and small. We also
publish book reviews and a new series of online programs.

www.ideasforleaders.com

The Center for the Future
of Organization (CFFO)

CFFO is an independent Think Tank and Research Center at the
Drucker School of Management at Claremont Graduate University.
The Center's mission is to deepen our understanding of new
capabilities that are critical to succeed in a digitally connected world,
and to support leaders and organizations along their transformational
journey.

In the tradition of Peter Drucker, the Center works across disciplines,
combining conceptual depth with practical applicability and ethical
responsibility, in close collaboration and connection with thought
leaders and practice leaders from academia, business, and consulting.

www.futureorg.org

DLQ Advisory Board

DevelopingLeaders
Quarterly

Milton Keynes UK
Ingram Content Group UK Ltd.
UKHW020748210324
439690UK00007B/123